Black Men
Speaking

Black Men
Speaking

EDITED BY

Charles Johnson and John McCluskey, Jr.

ι͹ο2Οι

ART BY

Jacob Lawrence

INDIANA UNIVERSITY PRESS

BLOOMINGTON & INDIANAPOLIS

Don Belton's "Voodoo for Charles" originally appeared in *Speak My Name,* © 1995 by Don Belton. Reprinted by permission of Beacon Press, Bouton.

Yusef Komunyakaa's poetry is reprinted here by permission of the author. It was originally published by Wesleyan University Press.

All works by Jacob Lawrence appear courtesy of the artist and Francine Seders Gallery, Seattle. Photo credit for *The Builders, Street Scene,* and *Overtime:* Chris Eden. Photo credit for *Munich Olympic Games, On the Way, The Workshop, To the Defense, Family,* and *People in Other Rooms:* Spike Mafford. Photo credit for *Wounded Man* and *Bread, Fish, Fruit:* Paul Macapia.

© 1997 BY INDIANA UNIVERSITY PRESS

THE PAPER USED IN THIS PUBLICATION MEETS THE MINIMUM REQUIREMENTS OF AMERICAN NATIONAL STANDARD FOR INFORMATION SCIENCES—PERMANENCE OF PAPER FOR PRINTED LIBRARY MATERIALS, ANSI Z39.48-1984.

MANUFACTURED IN THE UNITED STATES OF AMERICA

LIBRARY OF CONGRESS CATALOGING-IN-PUBLICATION DATA

BLACK MEN SPEAKING / EDITED BY CHARLES JOHNSON AND JOHN MCCLUSKEY, JR.
P.   CM.
ISBN 0–253–33259–1 (CLOTH : ALK. PAPER)
1. AFRO-AMERICAN MEN.   I. JOHNSON, CHARLES RICHARD, DATE.
II. MCCLUSKEY, JOHN, DATE.
E185.86.B5265   1997   95-53056
305.38896073—DC21

2   3   4   5   02   01   00   99   98   97

Contents

vi

Contents

Preface

This collection on the African American male experience was seven years in the making. Often it seemed that the gathering and editing of manuscripts might never be completed. That this book finally exists in finished form is a testament to the great patience of our contributors, all of whom I wish to thank, along with John Gallman, who in 1989 recognized the need for such a work long before other books about the dilemmas of black males went to press. And to my friend and fellow novelist John McCluskey, Jr., I want to express my deepest appreciation for carrying the weight of this project during the early nineties when I was too busy or overscheduled to work on it full-time. This *is* McCluskey's book, I believe, one that reflects the wisdom, professionalism, balance, steadiness, family orientation, and strength I have for twenty-six years admired in him and his remarkable wife Audrey (who greeted me always with kind words when I called their home at ridiculously late hours to pester John). Put simply, I would never have attempted co-editing a book as demanding as this one if the McCluskeys hadn't been there for me to lean on.

Obviously, this is not the first book to thematize the experiences of black men. Nor will it be the last, for the issues explored by our contributors are older than the American republic, reach back to the colonial era, slice deeply into every dimension of our public life in the present, and promise to be problems we will be addressing on the other side of the millennium. They are "black" issues, yes. And they center on African American males. But they are also profoundly human questions that go straight to the heart of culture and civilization in any era, and for any people. It is our hope that these essays, interviews, and poetry can function as guides—for our children, especially—as we approach a new century. If even one of our contributors serves that end (and I'm sure more than one will), then *Black Men Speaking* will have done its job well and justified our sojourn from its conception to completion.

Charles Johnson
Seattle, 1996

Preface

Introduction

Even though seven years have passed since we began soliciting essays from black men from very different backgrounds for this project, and despite the fact that so many have responded to what is regarded as a crisis in the black community, the problem has obviously become more acute than before, if the barrage of egregious statistics about black America is to be believed. For example, we are told that in 1989, one out of four young black men was entering, within, or emerging from the criminal justice system. In 1995 that number increased to one out of three. According to the NAACP Legal Defense and Educational Fund, on an average day in the United States, thirty-one black people are murdered—one every forty-six minutes. Homicide remains the leading cause of death for black males ages fifteen to nineteen. More blacks are murdered every six weeks in America than were lynched during the last 110 years. While black Americans make up 12 percent of the U.S. population, we accounted for nearly half those murdered in 1992. The reason for these high numbers is clearly firearms. Among those between the ages of fifteen and nineteen, guns were the second leading cause of death after traffic accidents between the years 1979 and 1989, according to the National Center for Health Statistics, claiming about a thousand black teenage males annually. Put another way, black men in inner-city neighborhoods are less likely to live to the age of sixty-five than men in Bangladesh.

And the statistics get worse. One of ten black Americans was the victim of a violent crime in 1995. A Justice Department survey conducted among 110,000 households reported that among blacks twelve or older, 111 of every 1,000 were victims of a violent crime—a rate 25 percent higher than for whites. There were 15.6 robberies for every 1,000 blacks, far exceeding the 4.7 rate for whites, and half of the murder victims in the country were black, 94 percent of whom were killed by other black people.

In 1991, William O'Hare, a social demographer at the University of Louisville, reported a fourfold increase since the late 1960s in the number of affluent black families earning $50,000 yearly. "You've got one segment moving up and the other stuck at the bottom," O'Hare said. These figures indicate that approximately one-third of black Americans, or 10 million people, are "stuck at the bottom," primarily in the inner cities. Census figures taken over the last decade present a disheartening economic picture. Blacks generally suffer twice the unemployment of whites and earn only half as much (56 percent). In 1986 blacks constituted 7 percent of professionals, 5 percent of managers, 8 percent of technicians, 17 percent of service workers, and 41 percent of domestic workers. At that time there were 339,000 black-owned businesses, 47 percent of which had gross annual receipts of less than $5,000. More recent figures compiled by Charlies James, publisher of the *African American Business and Employment Journal,* reveal that in 1996, for every 1,000 Arabs, 108 own a business; for every 1,000 Asians, 96; for every 1,000 whites, 64; and for every 1,000 blacks, the number is 9. Statistics gathered in 1984 indicated that the typical black household had a net worth of just $3,397, less than one-tenth that of the typical white household, which had a median net

Introduction

worth of $39,135, and nearly one-third of all black families (30.5 percent) reported that they owned no assets at all. More than half, 54 percent, had assets of less than $5,000.

Fifty-seven percent of black children live with only one parent, more than double the figure (21 percent) for white households. A decade ago, blacks accounted for 35 percent of separated Americans, 13 percent of those divorced, and 7 percent of those married. The percentage of low- and middle-income black males attending college dropped from 53 percent in 1976 to 28 percent in 1990, and today black college enrollment rates are at the level recorded for 1960, leading Jesse Jackson to say with accuracy that more black men are in prison than in college in the 1990s. Among black women, 70.3 percent are unmarried when their first child is born, and find themselves raising their children in fatherless homes. Added to this troubled portrait of the black American family is the finding by researchers that blacks are infected by the AIDS virus at six times the rate of whites.

In 1995, 827,440 black men in their twenties were in prison or jail or on probation or parole (30 percent of this group, compared to 7 percent for whites and 18 percent for Hispanics), many of them for drug violations. Although African Americans constitute only 12 percent of the population, blacks in 1995 accounted for 13 percent of monthly drug users, 35 percent of drug arrests, 55 percent of drug convictions, and 74 percent of those sentenced for drug violations. Recent reports reveal that 39 percent of California's black men in their twenties are in prison, in jail, or on probation. The findings released by the Center on Juvenile and Criminal Justice conclude that four out of ten young black male Californians were under the control of the courts, and that blacks are charged under the state's "three strikes" law at seventeen times the rate of whites, mainly for the sale or possession of crack cocaine.

Nationally, the drug trade has proven in the highly competitive economic environment of the 1980s and early 1990s to be devastating to the lives of young black males. Many of these men have low-paying regular jobs, a 1990 Rand Corporation study reported, but they can earn $24,000 a year moonlighting as dealers. A young dealer who works steadily can earn as much as $40,000 a year free of taxes. In Washington, D.C., the report stated, young black men brought in $354 million a year from drug sales, which is equal to one-fourth of the $1.2 billion earned by young black men from legitimate jobs.

None of these figures are lost on politicians, policy makers, and the shapers of public opinion. In the last two years, blacks— particularly black males—have been at the heart of the controversy that erupted in response to the book *The Bell Curve* by Charles Murray and Richard Herrnstein, a work that emphasizes a fifteen-point IQ differential between blacks and whites on standardized tests, and suggests in its conclusion that a "cognitive elite" will direct America's future from the boardrooms while those less genetically blessed may be best suited for blue-collar employment. The debate about blacks and IQ surfaced again in 1995's controversial *The End of Racism* by conservative Dinesh D'Souza, who says flat out that blacks are at the center of a "civilizational breakdown" fueled in large part by the barbarism of the black lower class and its celebration of the legendary "Bad Nigger" represented by Stagolee and gun-toting gangsta rap artists such as Ice T, Tupac Shakur, and 2-Live-Crew. Even Jesse Jackson has confessed to feeling fear when hearing footsteps behind him on a city street, then experiencing relief when, turning around, he discovers that the person behind him is white.

In "The Crisis of Public Order," (*Atlantic Monthly*, July 1995), Adam Walinsky predicts that of young black males in Washington, D.C., "70 percent . . . [will] be arrested before the age of thirty-five, and . . . 85 percent [will] be arrested at some point in their lives." He continues, grimly, to speculate that "in the year 2000 the black youths born in 1985 will turn fifteen. Three fifths of them were born to single mothers, many of

Introduction

whom were drug-addicted; one in fourteen will have been raised with neither parent at home; unprecedented numbers will have been subjected to beatings and other abuse; and most will have grown up amid the utter chaos pervading black city neighborhoods. It is supremely necessary to change the conditions that are producing such cohorts. But no matter what efforts we now undertake, we have already assured the creation of more very violent young men than any society can tolerate, and their numbers will grow inexorably for every one of the next twenty years." Walinsky argues that we need a larger police force to maintain public order, and concludes, "Let us not pretend that the bell tolls only for blacks; there is no salvation for one race alone, no hope for separate survival. At stake for all of us is the future of American cities, the promise of the American nation, and the survival of our Constitution and of American democracy itself."

Everywhere, it seems, black males are presented as uncivilized and subhuman. Old imagery dies hard. The black man as beast still retains great currency and acceptance in this culture. In the Bush campaign's exploitation of Willie Horton to frighten voters in 1988, in the racial slur about "Gorillas in the Mist" from the policeman who beat Rodney King as he would a dangerous animal, in the television footage of black male destructiveness during the Los Angeles riot, in the rise of the white supremacy movement in the last decade, in Pat Buchanan's attack on NEA for funding a film about gay black men (and ex-Klansman David Duke's startling though brief political success), in the sexual harassment charges against Clarence Thomas, who according to Anita Hill described himself as "Long Dong Silver," in the sexist "gangsta" lyrics offered by rap artists, in the gang-banging legions of Crips and Bloods, and even in the popular novels of several black women authors during the decade of the 1980s, we find the black male delivered to us as the stereotypical "Negro beast" so popular at the turn of the century—violent, sex-obsessed, irresponsible, and stupid.

There is no question that we are inundated by pessimistic statistics concerning black America. Since the days of slavery, the situation—and promise—of blacks in this country has been the subject of national debate. But what is most troubling is that in spite of the political and public relations gains of the civil rights movement in the 1950s and 1960s, old racist myths and stereotypes have returned in the generation born after 1970. Racism is more evident and, to a large degree, justified for many by the continuing problems of black American males. For examples of backlash we need look no further than the murder of a black couple by a white supremacist at Fort Bragg; the establishment by Sergeant Ed Kirste of the Los Angeles County Sheriff's Department of an organization to protect the rights of white male law-enforcement officers; the faux pas of CBS programming executive John Pike in reportedly saying that blacks are an important part of late-night television demographics because they stay up late since they have no jobs to go to in the morning, and that they prefer sketches to hour-long drama because their attention span is short; and the political capital gained by Republicans over the murder of a white Chicago woman on welfare by blacks who cut her unborn baby from her womb, as well as the story of a Detroit woman who sold her fifteen-year-old son to a drug dealer to pay for a $1,000 crack-cocaine debt.

Much of the new anti-black backlash we can attribute, of course, to worsening economic times in America. When competition for jobs is fierce, there is a tendency to demonize the racial Other who is one's competitor. Much of this is based on misinformation. According to a survey conducted recently by the U.S. Census Bureau, only 30 percent of whites believe that black economic and social inequality is due to past and present discrimination. Many believe that blacks are doing quite well, perhaps because they see affluent black entertainers so often in the media, and many feel that the black American population is larger (around 50 percent) than it actually is.

Introduction

Critics of black America such as D'Souza feel that the avalanche of statistics about black America add up to nothing less than empirical evidence of "black failure" in virtually every dimension of civilized life. In a 1993 study conducted by the Anti-Defamation League of B'nai B'rith, the researchers concluded that Americans between the ages of eighteen and thirty were more likely to hold anti-black views than their predecessors in the Baby Boom generation. Between the races, however, stereotyping works both ways. A survey commissioned by the National Conference of Christians and Jews in 1994 found that 33 percent of Latinos, 22 percent of Asians, and 12 percent of whites believed that "even if given a chance, African-Americans aren't capable of getting ahead." A recent survey reported that 35 percent of blacks believe that AIDS was likely the invention of white scientists plotting to annihilate the black population.

In their night march, statistics can be terrorists of the soul. They suggest a hopelessness, a lost cause for black and American communities. Yet there are glimmers of hope, slight divisions in the ranks that allow some dim light to show through. Let's reverse the odds: The majority of African Americans are not entering, within, or emerging from the criminal justice system. In 1980, 1,024,000 black Americans over the age of twenty-five reported four or more years of college education. In 1994, more than twice that number—2,337,000—reported the same level of education. More black Americans hold local, state, and national offices than ever before. In 1987, 424,165 black people owned and managed their own businesses; by 1992, that number had climbed to 620,912. The black presence in the world of the arts is as powerful as ever. During the last twenty years, black Americans have been nominated for or won a significant number of Pulitzer Prizes, National Book Awards, and Guggenheim and MacArthur fellowships. In the television and film industries, more African Americans are moving into the important positions of producer, director, and composer/author. Similarly, former successful athletes and businessmen are realizing the security that comes from full or partial ownership of professional sports franchises. Despite the assault by collected statistics, there are efforts to thwart pessimism and cynicism, though nothing tempers the fact of today's black-on-black violence.

Many panaceas have been proposed—among them more federal funding for youth and intervention programs, better schools and afterschool monitoring, and more role models. If we stand some distance away from the problem, it can seem overwhelming. Perhaps the real miracle—the hidden story in the statistics—is the way hope is kept alive in the various corners of the African American community. And we do not know enough yet about the heroic work done by grassroots organizations. Follow-up efforts after the Million Man March show the urgency of strengthening local networks in the spirit of ecumenism. In Indianapolis, for example, black nationalists, Marxists, Baptists, and Methodists (among others) have come together regularly to address problems and issues of common concern. Community workers such as Geoffrey Canada, author of *Fist Stick Knife Gun,* work with at-risk young men. Michael O'Neal, the author of an essay in this collection, is the director of Fathers, Inc., a Boston outreach agency committed to developing in young men the skills and responsibilities of fatherhood. MacArthur Fellow Joseph Marshall is the founder of the Omega Boys Club in San Francisco. He says that for every young black male he saves from crime and despair, he has saved three others as well—the person that young man might have killed or robbed, the young woman he might have impregnated, and the child they would have had. Might a national directory of such organizations be a useful first step? Furthermore, in this age of faxes and e-mail, might not community activists relay to one another what has worked and what has not worked with respect to, say, combating drugs in their neighborhoods? Would a Web site for constructive action be in order?

More programs are needed along the lines of Seattle's Black

Introduction

Dollar Days Task Force's Campaign 5000, which has raised $220,000 from 5,000 individuals contributing $200 each and 500 corporations that pledged $1,000 apiece. The task force's goal is to raise $1.5 million to provide short-term loans to black entrepreneurs. In March of 1996, with civil-rights activist Dick Gregory on hand for the ceremony, the first of three loans was made—$6,000 to a young man to help start a hazardous-waste hauling business, $2,000 to a restaurant owner who plans to provide a delivery service to her customers, and another $2,000 to the Ghanaian owner of an African-theme market to broaden his inventory. Of the program Gregory remarked, "I don't see anything that's going to end the struggle other than when masses of people come together and pool their money for economic ventures."

How do we survive in these times and into the future? How do we forge bonds strong enough to sustain a community? How do we view one another? And how do we view ourselves individually? Do we allow the efflorescence of many different cultural styles within the black community itself? How do we define "blackness"? Maleness and femaleness? The family? And should we even try to define these things? The essays that we requested for this book are meant to sustain a dialogue on these questions with readers and with other works. Clearly black men have reared families, loved their wives, found their gods, contributed to the building of this nation, and created lasting works of art. And certainly this was not done alone. Wives, lovers, children, parents, memories—all these have played and will continue to play profound roles in our future. It is important to remember that not all survival strategies are revealed in public. Many are transmitted quietly and are not recorded or expressed in institutional ways. However, at this eleventh hour of the twentieth century, we need to know more about the range of these rituals and how for each unique situation we face they can be improvised upon—extended, elaborated, refined, as author Albert Murray once put it. Again, we need to know what works

Introduction

and what does not in constructing healthy relationships on the private, social, and political levels. We need to learn these things and pass them along.

During and since slavery, the passing along has been done in many ways—through conversations over meals, through sermons and song, through dialogues in barbershops and pool halls. The forms have been many, the messages often varying in sounds reflective of region and class. The point here is the importance of the transmission of our lived experience and that of our black predecessors to counter the weight of falsified versions of who we have been, what we are, and what we can be. Though letters to down-home friends belied his public address, Richard Wright shaped and presented a bleak and lonely view in 1945. His justly notorious passage in the second chapter of *Black Boy* (New York: Harper and Row, 1945, p. 33) can cast a pall:

> Whenever I thought of the essential bleakness of black life in America, I knew that Negroes had never been allowed to catch the full spirit of Western civilization, that they lived somehow in it but not of it. And when I brooded upon the cultural barrenness of black life, I wondered if clean positive tenderness, love, honor, loyalty and the capacity to remember were native to man. I asked myself if these human qualities were not fostered, won, struggled and suffered for, preserved in ritual from one generation to another.

As read by Ralph Ellison in his fine review essay "Richard Wright's Blues," the stress in the passage should lie with the conscious ritual of keeping important life-affirming values before us. Our very humanness depends upon these forms and expressive gestures.

Since the mid-nineteenth century, false sciences and the emerging and earnest social sciences have listed the supposed pathologies of black American life. Much of early black social-science scholarship was given over to explaining, clarifying, and defending the national black community. Think here of Du Bois, E. Franklin Frazier, Drake and Cayton, and Carter G. Woodson. At the same time, African Americans have served as

Introduction

arbiters of national taste. In terms of examining American popular culture in the nineteenth century, the work of Constance Rourke (*American Humor: A Study of the National Character and Roots of American Culture*) and Robert Toll (*Blacking Up*) has been priceless. Each examines the role of African Americans, especially males, in national humor and in minstrelsy and musical theater. Each argues for the centrality of the African American presence to national character.

Visit any mall and check out the sneakers, the baseball caps, and the music coming through loudly on walkmans in the hands of non–African Americans. It may not be the only image of the African American male, but it is somebody's very popular version. Similarly, eavesdropping in chain record stores can also be instructive. This is not to make light of pathologies and self-destructive tendencies where they occur. (We repeat: Nothing tempers the fact of black-on-black violence.) But it is to suggest a complex relationship that is often ignored in our discussions of image, cultural power, and survival strategies. It is intriguing that the celebrated media attention given to Clarence Thomas and Anita Hill and to O.J. Simpson has prompted national discussions on the problem of sexual harassment in the workplace and on domestic violence.

The point here is that the African American male, while generally lacking proportionate social and economic power, has nevertheless played and continues to play a central role in the workings of the national psyche. To be sure, there are distortions, misrepresentations, and omissions; we know what many are. (In this election year, welfare and police-arming issues will be colored darkly.) It is in the face of the latter narratives that the true and complex stories must be told and retold.

In our effort to present a bit of that complexity, we solicited essays from a broad range of individuals. It was not our intention to collect statements only from academics or artists. We asked each for a description of major issues facing African American males at this time and what solutions each would suggest for the near future. From their vantage points, ranging from physician to community organizer, from journalist to the recently unemployed, they gave their answers and passed on their truths and perspectives. Dr. Wilbert Jordan, a Los Angeles internist, offered a parable with insightful commentary. Joseph Scott contributed a moving memoir of his father. Pianist, composer, and educator Ellis Marsalis commented on public education, diversity, and discipline. These are just a few examples of the wide spectrum of backgrounds presented here. Their sounds are distinct and their melodies often surprising. If the harmonies of the whole are less than Ellingtonian, the maestros knew the risks.

John McCluskey, Jr. Charles Johnson
Indiana University University of Washington

Introduction

Black Men
Speaking

The Builders

1. Making a Way Out of No Way

DADDY WAS PLAIN SCARED OF WHITE FOLKS

My Daddy was a soft-spoken gentle diminutive man, a little too gentle for my liking. He would rather pray for than beat up white people who called him names and denied him service. Instead of cursing them, he'd say to us, "Dem white folks will kill you if you don't watch yo mouth."

After he saw us talking to white people just any kind of way, he'd tell us stories about how white mobs used to maul and lynch young black men even if they only raised their hands to strike back in self-defense. He talked about men he'd known when he was growing up in rural Georgia who had been lynched, and he'd tell us he knew his "place" and that we had to learn "our place." This wasn't our experience, so we thought that he was just plain scared of white people. He could not convince us to show deference to white people just because they were white. They didn't have to be honest or morally respectable. No, they just had to be white and they were due our respect. Racial respect.

We lived in a Polish ghetto in Detroit, Michigan. We couldn't fathom this "our place" stuff. Virtually all of our schoolmates were white. And for a long time, all of our neighbors were white.

We were not going to concede honor and rank to any white peers just because they were white.

"That don't make any sense to me," I'd say. "You da one who ain't got no sense," he'd say.

My Daddy lived before Martin Luther King was known, so My Daddy was the first advocate of nonviolence and passive resistance I knew. Martin Luther King could not compare to him; My Daddy was the ultimate pacifist in the face of white people. I was not proud of My Daddy for either his philosophy or his behavior.

My Daddy said, "Yes Suh" and "No Suh" to all white males, old and young. They could call him "nigger" or "darky," but he would just tip his hat and say, "Yes Suh."

When my older brothers' and my white friends came to our house after football practice or after playing basketball in the alley behind the house, My Daddy would say, "Yes Suh" and "No Suh" to them. We were embarrassed and they were embarrassed by such displays of racial deference, since we kicked their butts regularly. My brothers' response was to warn their white friends not to insist on such archaic racial etiquette from them. If they insisted, they had better be prepared for a very rude physical awakening. As far as my brothers and I were concerned, the racial etiquette of the South was ancient history, and the North was a new day.

Not surprisingly, My Daddy never took any one of us "Down South" after we grew up and wore knee pants. Emmett Till's lynching distressed him so much that he'd just look at us after that with sad, wet eyes all the time.

From watching My Daddy deal with white people for the first ten years of my life, I concluded that he was just plain scared of white folks.

NOT SEEING EYE TO EYE

"Boy, you cain't see where you headed? You headed for no good. Don't you know that white folks will kill you? You talk to

JOSEPH W. SCOTT

white folks like you white. Don't you know yo place? You gonna learn the hard way—someday." Shaking his head, "You so damn hardheaded."

Sometimes he glared at me so hard and long that tears would well up in his eyes, causing him to blink as fast as he could in order to use up the tears before they dropped over the rims of his eyes.

As he stared at me, he seemed to be trying to see inside my head. And the more he saw, the more hurt and frustrated he became. I could see in his grimaces that he could not fathom my thinking, my reasoning. I was his lucky son—his seventh son. But I was acting in some unlucky ways.

From my standpoint, My Daddy had to be wrong about this "white place"/"black place" stuff. My school and neighborhood experiences had taught me that blacks had the same rights as white people. My face-to-face experiences of kicking white playmates' butts had also told me that whites were not innately superior. In fact, my experiences had taught me that many of them were not even *equal* to me or to the average street "bro" I knew. What I saw was that more whites than blacks needed protection. What I saw was that my school grades had also told me that in head-to-head competition, I was getting better grades than the majority of white boys or girls my age.

But My Daddy's experiences were different. During his life-time, he had seen that whites owned and controlled virtually everything that could be owned, and that they determined black people's choices and opportunities, and not the other way around.

But my growing up in this little Polish ghetto, playing foot-ball against white boys and beating them on the playing field and courts, taught me that whites were not as omnipotent as My Daddy described them. So I continued to be defiant of the racial customs and courtesies to which My Daddy wanted me to conform. I could not see the world through his eyes, and he could not see the world through mine. And so I continued to believe that My Daddy was congenitally scared of white people.

3

HIS TURNING POINT

One day when I was about eleven years old, a group of us children were playing baseball in the alley behind our garages. Tempers flared as they sometimes do among children, but we started no fights. Someone hit a ball over my head, and I went running down the alley to chase the rolling baseball. All of a sudden I heard my younger brother screaming and crying, and I turned around to see a boy who was my age and size on top of my smaller brother beating him unmercifully. I ran back, pulled the boy off my brother, and began to beat him up. He broke away and ran into his yard, across the alley from our house, and called his father in a panic. His father came running out, and the boy told him that the "niggers" had beaten him up. His father immediately ran over to me and started swinging his fist at me. I dodged the blows, and at the same time told my little brother to run and get one of my older brothers. I picked up the baseball bat and held the man at a distance, waiting to hear one of my brothers coming. To my surprise, My Daddy came out of the gate first, and when I saw him, I knew I was in trouble. From everything I knew up to that time, My Daddy would rather whip me than confront a white man. My stomach sank with the feeling of defeat, and I felt that now I was facing both a beating from the white man and a beating from My Daddy.

However, much to my surprise, My Daddy came out not with a belt but with a little tiny pocketknife that he used for cleaning his nails. His fists seemed so tight, his posturing so bold and aggressive, that our white neighbor forgot that all My Daddy had was a penknife, and the white man started pleading, apologizing, and backing away into his yard.

About then, Monda (we called my mother that) came out— a minute or so behind my father. She was even more angry and aggressive. Her mother-hen protectiveness was exceedingly pronounced. She pushed my father aside, grabbed this man by his shirt collar, pulled him back into the alley, pushed him up

JOSEPH W. SCOTT

against his garage, and held him there with all of her 225 pounds. She instructed my sister who was two years older than I to jump over the fence, run down this man's son, bring him back out in the alley, and beat him up in front of his father. My sister obeyed without hesitation, as we were all trained to do.

Now, as I look back, I do not know whether My Daddy would have used that little knife, but I learned that this fervently nonviolent Christian man had his limits with white men. In the past, he had revealed only his fears of white men, never his pent-up rage. I did not know that in all of his praying for white people, he was praying away tons of rage.

I believe that he was distressed about having to confront a white man in such a manner, but I think he was also distressed at the thought of having to live with himself and my mother had he not defended his children in this situation. I also believe with all my heart that his love for us overcame his fear of white people at that moment.

OUR NEIGHBORHOOD

The Polish ghetto in which I was raised consisted mostly of newly arrived immigrants and their children. It was a separately incorporated city, but an island within the geographical perimeter of Detroit.

Pole Town had its own schools and government, its own family culture and communal organization. It had donut shops, butcher shops, bakeries, delicatessens, and haberdasheries, nearly all owned and/or controlled by Poles. The private schools, the Catholic churches, the social clubs, the community hospitals, the radio stations, and the newspaper were mostly Polish too. And on the streets of this little Polish village, mostly Polish could be heard.

The Poles prepared different but wonderful-tasting foods. Within the array of little mom-and-pop stores were barrels of imported Polish hams, sour dill pickles, pickled herring, smoked

Making a Way Out of No Way

herring, sauerkraut, and other Polish delicacies with powerfully pungent smells. The smoked garlic-studded sausages, brown and black rye breads, purple eggplant, and green tomatoes were uncommonly delicious. The signs on the foods and produce in the stores were in Polish, necessitating that we learn some Polish words to survive. We learned the Polish word for "nigger" first. But few black men learned enough Polish to speak it fluently. I used to see them standing on the corners with Polish men, talking a mile a minute, laughing with gusto, and joking with nuance and subtlety. I grew up wanting to be just like these black men—ordinary garbage men, factory workers, construction workers—who had taken the time and effort to master the spoken Polish language. They were role models to me, and I tried to imitate them. As fate would have it, I became a better garbage man than a Polish-language speaker.

Our family was the first black family to move onto our block; in fact, we were the first black people to move into this entire area. On the blocks immediately to the south, north, and east, there were no other black families. We were surrounded on three sides by European peoples—mostly Polish—and on the fourth side we were hemmed in by a Chevrolet factory—the gears and axle and foundry divisions.

Ironically, even though these new immigrants were not even citizens yet, they thought that we should not be living in this area. And even though they knew very little English, they held enough prejudice in their hearts to actively oppose our moving in. My three oldest brothers told me how the Polish boys ran them home from school during the first few days after our family moved in. But my mother, who had little patience with disrespectful white people, tired of that quickly.

One day she stood on the porch, her massive arms folded high across her chest and the ironing cord in her right hand, as my three eldest brothers came running down the street out of breath and started up the steps. They said that they "skidded" to a stop. Well, I don't know how you skid on bare wood in rubber

JOSEPH W. SCOTT

tennis shoes, unless you are really streaking, but "skidded" is how they described it. My mother stood rock firm, unfolded her arms, drew back the ironing cord as if to snap a whip, and said, "You can take a beatin' from me or you can fight 'em and beat 'em real good." Knowing my mother's ironing-cord whippings, they didn't even see that as a choice. My mother was one of those "Big Mamas." She was short, stocky, broad-shouldered, and much stronger than the average factory man. She could do anything a southern rural black man could do: She could chop down trees, hunt rabbits with a shotgun, ride mules bareback, make whiskey, lay bricks, do carpentry and plumbing, and lift heavy logs. She absolutely never said to us children, "Wait 'til yo fatha comes home" to repair something. She just told us to go to the hardware store to get the supplies, and together we fixed whatever had to be fixed, or lifted whatever had to be moved.

She was only 5'4", but she was an intimidating woman of such will and strength that we were convinced she was eager to do battle. She could grab us by the collar and hold on without our being able to pull away, even though we were strong, growing teenage boys who played junior high and high school football.

So my brothers said that they jumped back down the stairs and kicked "white butts" in all directions, up and down the street. The next day and all the days after, they went to school and came home unmolested, not even challenged. They had won the right to live in peace in this Polish neighborhood, but more important, they had also learned a little manhood—from my mother.

OUR HOUSE

I was born during the Great Depression. At that time in Pole Town, no one had to be unemployed to see his toes even with shoes on.

Our tiny wood frame cottage was not much shelter during

the Michigan winters. The winds came into our living rooms and bedrooms any time they wanted and stayed there as long as they wanted without paying any rent.

Five of us brothers slept in the same bedroom, three of us in one bed and two in another, and each night I had to fight for my twelve inches of space on our sagging tattered mattress, which was a family heirloom. With such wear and tear, the chinches visited us often.

Huge Norway rats resided inside the walls, and three of the regulars lived inside the wall right next to our bed. These rats thought they were entitled to bed space, too. They played tag in the walls every night, waiting for us to go to sleep. Then they could push the rag out of the hole above our bed and play tag on us—on their way to the kitchen to look for anything we might have dropped on the floor or left unlocked. Because spare food was hard to find at our house, night after night they came back across the bed angry, probably wondering how human beings could live with such scarcity and wanting even more after this kind of visit to take a bite out of us.

One night we decided to stop the rats' bold trekking. We tied one string from the light bulb hanging from the ceiling in the middle of the room to the doorknob, and we tied a second string from that string to our bed. All we had to do was pull this last string, and the light would come on and the door would close at the same time. We put newspaper on the floor leading out the door so that we could hear the rats leaving and returning. We waited with brooms, mops, and sticks until they went out to the kitchen and came running back in across the paper. When they came in, we pulled the string. The light came on, the door closed behind them, and the rumble was on. We fought for an hour or so, with the rats jumping up into the bedsprings so that we wouldn't be able to trap them on the floor or in a corner. We finally rolled up the mattresses and used them and the corner to trap the rats one at a time. But they fought bravely—they did not give up without a helluva fight. They stood up on their hind

JOSEPH W. SCOTT

legs as if to box with the broom and mop handles being swung at them. We were victorious that night.

DADDY'S HANDS AND GLOVES

When I was growing up, My Daddy's hands and work gloves spoke volumes to me. More often than not, his gloves were just patches of rags and cowhide held together by steel-like threads which refused to let go even if you tried to pull the gloves apart. Blackened by a combination of thick axle grease and black foundry sand, they were as stiff as cardboard when he left our house on cold mornings to go to work at the hammer shop. These gloves exposed as much of his hands as they covered even after he warmed them up on his furnace.

The automobile industry is an up-and-down business. During the up times, My Daddy crossed the street every workday morning to go to the hammer shop across from our tiny wood-framed house. He went through the watchman's search, then entered the hammer shop, where he pounded out gears and axles for Chevrolet cars and trucks.

I once saw his hammer, and it was as big as our house. Every one of its downward blows shook the ground below and even shook our house across the street. I saw the furnaces that heated the raw steel before it was pounded into a gear or axle. The air around the hammer had to be over 120 degrees. The steel itself was indescribably hot; when the heat-treat man opened the furnace to pull out the glowing steel, even he grimaced at the blast of heat coming out of it. Even his tongs seemed to protest and writhe at having to grasp that red-hot steel.

My Daddy's only protection against this skin-searing, hair-singeing heat was his ragged gloves. Because they were worn threadbare, he flinched each time he grasped the giant tongs to turn and twist the steel until the right shape appeared under the repeated earthshaking blows. As I watched him hold on blow after blow, with sparks of steel chips flying everywhere, absorb-

9

ing the heat and the shock, I imagined that hell must be kind of like this place.

My Daddy and his gloves were on the one end of those tongs, and the red-hot steel was on the other. And if the tongs were having such a hard time, My Daddy had to be in even more pain. The gloves had to be only psychological help, because they were more gone than there.

His callused hands showed the evidence. His skin wore away wherever it was exposed and came into contact with the tongs. Where my hands had the normal creases at each joint, his hands had thick, hardened, discolored, jagged-edged calluses, with bloody cracks in the calluses where normal creases would be.

Every morning at daybreak before he left the house to go to his hammer, he fell down upon his knees and closed his bruised and battered hands in prayer, thanking the Lord for "anotha day's jo'rney." He'd say, "I thank you for wakin' me up this mornin' closed in my right mind, wit' duh blood runnin' warm in my veins, and duh use and aktividies of ma limbs. I thank you for watchin' ova me yestaday whilst I was on my job. You kep' one han' ova me and one han' unda me, and you kep' me from faintin' and fallin' by the wayside. And I'm thankin' you for it. I'm askin' you to go wit' me t'day whilst I'm on my job. Keep yo strong armor of patection around me. Keep me outa all hurt, harm, and danga." After praying loudly and fervently for about thirty minutes, he would raise himself up and walk across the street, carrying those ragged gloves for protection—such as it was.

Lifting skin-cooking steel with good gloves would have been punishment, but lifting that steel with the gloves My Daddy had was torture, at least to me. When he came home, he sat down at the head of the table, closed his callused, cracked hand, blessed the food, and blessed "the ones who p'pared the food." I felt a special feeling whenever those rough hands touched me gently.

As I grew, I became aware that the cost of work gloves com-

JOSEPH W. SCOTT

peted with the cost of feeding, sheltering, and keeping warm ten children and a wife. My Daddy's ragged gloves symbolized too much for me to completely fathom, but I did understand that they represented high sacrifices.

SHOE REPAIR

My Daddy was a "doing" kind of man. He believed that a "real" man should be a doer. When I told him I was studying sociology, he asked, "What can you do with it?" I said, "Well, I don't know yet, but I know a lot." He asked, "Can you fix shoes with it? Can you do the washing, ironing, cooking, sewing, painting, or anything like that with it?" My answer was, "No, sir." Again, he walked away shaking his head.

With ten children to feed, shelter, and clothe, My Daddy always had to be doing odd jobs to make a few dollars. His side occupation was fixing shoes. He repaired the work shoes of fellow workers.

On his way home from the factory, he stopped by the trash bin and looked in. If he found pieces of discarded leather pulley belts about six inches wide and a half-inch thick and two or three feet long, he brought them home. The leather was jet black from old engine oil that had spilled on it over the months, and it made great waterproof soles, which is what the hammer shop workers needed, since the hammers were water-cooled and leaked water which stood in puddles on the factory floor around these machines.

My Daddy had an old shoe last with interchangeable "feet" of various sizes for holding the shoes, which came to him in sizes ranging from six to fourteen. The shoes he brought home to fix were always old and tattered, with holes worn in the soles. I used to think that My Daddy would have to be a magician to repair those shoes. With his special leather-cutting knife he cut out the soles and the heels to the exact sizes, then tacked them in place using hundreds of tacks in perfect rows. He finished each

Making a Way Out of No Way

shoe by hand-sanding the leather edges until they were smooth as new leather. Finally, he put shoe polish on these dirty, greasy worn shoe tops and brushed them until some semblance of a shine appeared. After three hours of work on these shoes, he took them to the owner and collected maybe $1.50 a pair. This money could buy some work gloves to protect his hands from the searing heat, or some rubbing alcohol or liniment to soothe his aching arms, legs, feet, or back. Or the money could be used for food or utilities—and usually was.

FINDING A WAY OUT OF NO WAY

What does a black ex-sharecropper with ten children to feed do when he is "up North," far away from his brothers and sisters, and the foreman at the automobile plant where he works gives him the dreaded layoff slip just as winter snow is coming on strong? Does he desert his hungry children, so the children can go on public aid? Or steal some food from the corner grocery store knowing that he will surely be identified if caught, and knowing that the whole family's honor could go down the toilet with one desperate act?

Or does he mope around the house feeling sorry for himself and in a rage slap his children to cover his embarrassment when he sees them fighting over a single piece of day-old hard corn-bread? Or does he pickle his brain with alcohol at a bar down the block in an attempt to escape momentarily the angry eyes of his wife and the saddened eyes of his toddlers? Or does he come home from the bar and attempt to whip everyone in his little corner of the world?

During times such as these, My Daddy committed none of these affronts. My Daddy got down on his knees and stayed down on his knees a mighty long time, praying as fervently and as plaintively as he could.

"You said when we need you, to call yo name.
Well, Lord, I need you right now.

JOSEPH W. SCOTT

I know you busy, Lord,
But whilst you on yo rounds,
Stop by here, O Lord, and see about your servant right here.
I'm down here in this world, with trouble on every side,
And I have to go along with an aching heart sometimes.
I have to shed tears sometimes.
I know you know all about it.
You know all things.
I need you right now, Lord, right now,
And I am depending on yo word.
You told me a long time ago that your word would never fail.
So please have mercy on me, Lord.
Yo mercy will solve all my problems.
I do believe that all power is in yo hands:
You a doctor who can heal sick wounds.
You a lawyer who never lost a case.
You can open doors no man can open.
You can close doors no man can close.
You can speak, and man lives.
You can speak, and man dies.
You bread in the time of hunger.
You water in the time of thirst.
You light in the time of darkness.
You shelter in the time of storms.
You a shield in the time of battle.
I do believe you can make a way out of no way."

My Daddy prayed an improvised prayer like this one for twenty or thirty minutes, his pain and grief so evident that a hush would fall over the house so completely that even the rats in the walls grew quiet. After praying, he would get up from his knees, slowly lifting one knee at a time, and straighten up his back so very deliberately that I used to think he might fall forward on his face again. He would put on his moth-eaten felt hat and leave the house. In a few hours, he would come back with two or three loaves of bread, or a sack of white potatoes, or

Making a Way Out of No Way

a five-pound bag of cornmeal and a bucket of Alaga syrup, or a box of ends of lunch meats, or something else he had scraped up by sure honest effort.

His faith in God caused him to sublimate his destructive potential into positive presentations of his God-directed self.

MY FIRST RITE OF PASSAGE

At the tender age of nine, I experienced the first of many rites of passage to manhood through work. Both my father and my mother had more than subtly intimated on more than one occasion that I should go out and get a job to help support the family.

The Great Depression was still in full force in our family, and for that matter in our whole neighborhood. The need for money to cover the family's necessities was the suppertime topic each day. Even when my father worked full-time, and seven days a week, he earned a poverty-level income only. We were not living at the poverty level just because he now had ten children. Even when he had only one child, his wages were poverty-level wages. So with twelve mouths to feed, his meager wages made more noticeable the income that was needed to survive at or above the poverty line. Our collective family needs were greater than our collective family income, and his income alone was never enough to supply us with all of the shoes, rubber boots, caps, sweaters, trousers, scarves, socks, coats, heat, electricity, burial insurance, and bedrooms we needed. Notwithstanding that fact, My Daddy always put food on the table.

Still, no matter how long and how hard my father worked (and he worked as hard as it was humanly possible to do and not die), his paycheck from Chevrolet was never large enough in any week even to cover the cost of the quantity of food we ten children ate. Our daily bread was literally bought on credit at a little corner grocery store owned and run by "Polish Joe," but our grocery bill was so large and our money so short, we could make

JOSEPH W. SCOTT

only partial payments on the bill, as some people today pay for purchases in installments.

During the first eighteen years of my life, we never paid *off* our food bill; we only paid *on* it. We were able to pay it off only after I had finished high school and several of us were working in the auto plants, all contributing 40 percent of our income to our parents.

Even though Polish Joe's prices were higher than those at the A&P supermarket, we had no other choice but to shop at his store. He and he alone was kind enough to extend us credit. During my childhood, we seldom shopped for our daily food on a cash-and-carry basis because my parents continued to buy overpriced food on credit, and continued to pray to God to make a way for us to pay this grocery bill which was sometimes growing faster than our collective income. With a promise and a prayer, and with pride and penny-pinching during these depressing times, my parents religiously avoided and aggressively refused welfare. They were too proud to live on "commodities" even though they "qualified" for them as both "the truly needy" and "the deserving poor." The welfare people said that we were not lazy, not willfully idle, and not poor from self neglect.

JUNKING

Rather than go on welfare, even though we needed to go on it and qualified for it, My Daddy taught all of us boys how to go "junking." He built a large pushcart out of discarded automobile wheels, an automobile axle, and old lumber. This box-like contraption served as an oversized buggy, with which we went up and down alleys picking through rubbish and garbage for anything that could be recycled. Recycling centers bought tin cans, newspapers, pop bottles, zinc lids, aluminum pots and pans, copper tubing, and old rags by the pound. After days and days of "junking" and days and days of sorting and accumulating, we would sell the items and make a few nickels here and a few nickels there—enough to buy a couple of loaves of bread, or a peck of potatoes, or five pounds of flour or white cornmeal, or an electric bulb, or the like.

I did not know it at the age of six when I started "junking," but My Daddy was teaching us how to "make a way out of no way." By the time I went to college, I felt that once I was accepted, I would finish because I knew how to scuffle—that is, how to make a way out of no apparent visible means of acquiring an income. No stealing, no snatching of purses, no dice playing, no other forms of gambling. Just plain honest work was the way My Daddy represented "making it" in life to us.

THE MEASURE OF MANHOOD IN MY FAMILY

My father gently started encouraging me to look for a job to help the family out, and he did it in a most extraordinary way. It was a cold winter day. The snow was knee-deep for a boy of my size (I was undersized at nine). We had run out of the chunks of coal which we fed to our potbellied stove in order to heat the house. My Daddy told me to find a burlap sack and follow him. We left the house and went out into the deep snow, walking down the alley toward the railroad yard. We trudged quite a long way until we came to eight or ten sets of railroad tracks. He started walking up one set of tracks and down another, with me literally following in his footsteps. Every once in a while, he would spot some black coal—invisible to my untrained eye—hidden by snow, and his face would fill up with glee. With each precious piece we went through the ritual of dusting off the snow and putting it into our burlap sacks. "Kinda like fin'ing money," he would say. We walked and walked for miles, it seemed, until we had two sacks full of coal.

The coal had fallen off the overfilled boxcars which passed this way en route to the steel-treating and foundry furnaces at the Chevrolet plant. All year long My Daddy had noticed that

JOSEPH W. SCOTT

the boxcars were overloaded and that pieces of coal occasionally fell off on the ground. Now it was winter and we had come back to find the "nigger's gold."

For the longest time, I did not understand this term, "nigger's gold," in its full meaning. But as I came of age and learned to recognize and know racism, I also came to understand that the "yellow gold" was reserved for white people, and coal, "nigger's gold," if we could find it, was reserved for black people. In this way I learned that everything in this world had a class or race meaning attached to it. Nothing was just neutral in this society.

From repeated days and cold, dark winter evenings of scavenging like this with My Daddy, the family needs became more and more apparent. The need for more family income, and thus the need for me to find a job to help support the family, became slap-in-the-face clear.

My Daddy did not explain in long and dramatic words; men of his time were men of few words. They were men of action. They showed the way. They led. After leading me on so many trips to hunt and gather coal, he did not have to "explain" anything. Our family's need for money was great, and my need for my parents' esteem was just as great.

I would no longer be just an income consumer; I would also become an income producer. I would now go out and find an afterschool job and work on Saturdays or Sundays too if I could. But at the age of nine, how does a 4'9" black boy in a "foreign country," wearing mismatched socks and patched trousers, interview for a job and be acceptable when he looks like a ragamuffin?

Well, my parents told me, "You wander from sto to sto, from houst to houst, and garage to garage, and you axe them folks for work, and you'll fine a Good Samaritan on yo road."

And so, at the age of nine, I went out in the streets and alleys of Pole Town looking for work. I don't remember how long it took, but one day I wandered down an alley and walked past an auto repair operation in a garage. I asked if they needed a boy to

Making a Way Out of No Way

clean up the garage. They said yes and hired me on the spot. (My Daddy's prayers had been answered once again.) One of my tasks was to pick up tools and clean the dirt and grease off of them, then hang them on the tool board in their pre-marked places so the mechanics could begin each workday without the delay of having to look for any equipment. Another of my tasks was to sweep the garage each evening. For this work I was paid twenty-five cents a day, which was enough to pay for my socks, some soap, and even my shoes after six or seven months of work. When my playmates were about roller skating, or playing baseball, or standing on the corners joking around, I was on my job thinking of my family's survival, and knowing that I was indeed making a difference.

But there was another lesson I had to learn in all of this success: None of my earnings was mine to keep or to use at my discretion. Another custom in my family was that the youngest children did not keep any of what they earned. All of our income was turned over to my mother, who used the money for the common welfare of all. "One for all and all for one" was the norm. The family as a whole was more important than any one individual. Income was not individualized or privatized. Income was familial, even communal if need be. My Daddy did not even cash his own paychecks: He brought them home to my mother. But I had a hard time with this norm, so I had to learn this value of familism the hard way: I protested once that my parents were not spending my earnings on me. My mother said to me, "You da mose selfish chile I have." It hurt me so badly, I gasped for something to say, but what *could* I say? I had been working for weeks without once keeping anything. Calling me "selfish" knocked nearly all the wind out of me. But in the face of overwhelming needs, where our collective income never exceeded outgo, what could I say in defense of myself? I guess I *was* being selfish. I never protested aloud again. I dutifully worked and gave all of my earnings to my mother. She decided when and what to buy me; she decided what shoes, socks, trousers, shirts, or boots I needed and when I needed them.

JOSEPH W. SCOTT

Sometimes I was leaving my toeprints in the sand, but I got new shoes on her time, not mine. At other times I went to school wearing mismatched socks or socks so long I had to fold them underneath my feet inside my shoes, but I got new socks on her time as well. No matter how dire my personal needs were, I never asked again.

There were not many direct material rewards from earning money, but there were other, more intrinsic rewards. In our family, manhood was partly measured by our personal contributions to the family income. By this norm, I became as much a man as some of my older brothers after I secured a job earning money for the family. For example, my parents began to treat me more like an adult. They shared with me more confidential information about family finances. They asked my opinions about important family matters. They allowed me to read official notices and letters. They sent me on diplomatic errands to lawyers and other important people. My Daddy sent me to Polish Joe's with important messages such as "Tell Polish Joe I cannot pay on the groc'y bill this week. Tell him I'll pay on it next payday." My mother sent me to uncles with messages like "Tell Uncle Lonnie I need ten dollars right now," or "Go over to Uncle Joe's and tell him to send me a piece of cured hog jowl for my supper today." I was rewarded with insider status in family matters for my financial contributions.

Another custom was that the older you were, the higher up on the hog or the chicken you ate. "Eating low" meant that you ate the feet, the necks, the backs, the heads, or the tails, whether it was the hog or the chicken. "Eating high up" meant eating the other parts. In our family, chronological age in and of itself carried with it both privileges and obligations, and one of the privileges was eating higher on the hog and chicken. But contributing income to the family pool also earned one the right to eat higher. My material reward for contributing to my family's income was that I was given slices of hog shoulder or slices of ham, chicken thighs, wishbones, and breast pieces.

In sum, contributing to my family's income earned me a

special place in my parents' hearts and new status in our family system. Nevertheless, when I look back on it, I had to grow up much too fast, and miss out on the innocence of childhood. I was already a manchild at nine.

HOMEWORK TIME

My Daddy set an example for homework. After supper, especially on long winter evenings, he took out his Bible and sat and read near the potbellied stove in our dining room. He vocalized as he read, and he struggled with every word. But he pressed on and persevered and read those passages over and over again, to memorize each word of each passage. He read them aloud to himself, and he sang them aloud to himself in what is called Down South "long meter." He used his Bible study at home to enable him to get up in church and recite Bible verses and sayings, and through those acts he gained recognition and esteem from his peers for his literacy. For his generation, he was the exception. Not many men of his origin and age had his degree of "edication."

Most of the time the dining room had a single light bulb, hanging from an electric cord in the middle of the room. It was turned on by a string hanging down, out of the reach of the small children. Quite often we could not afford lights for each room, so we moved the light bulb from room to room. We had to compete with one another for the bulb, and God bless the person who dropped it. Most of the time I did not assume the risk of handling the bulb, so I went to bed and used whatever light was showing through the bedroom doorway from the dining room.

My Daddy had only the most basic education, just rudimentary skills and knowledge. Nevertheless, he publicly displayed to us children how important learning was, and how one had to daily dedicate oneself to the endless pursuit of self-improvement. He showed us that institutional deprivation was no ex-

JOSEPH W. SCOTT

cuse for not teaching oneself the skills, knowledge, and conduct that one needs in life.

My Daddy impressed upon me the importance of formal education in another way. He had gone to school for only a part of three years in rural Georgia, where harvest time took precedence over school time when the plantation owners called for labor to work in the cotton fields. Still, during his three partial years, he had learned some ditties, rhymes, and jubilee. He recited them hundreds of times, to impress us with his learning and to show us he was "edicated." He also recited one or two lines of a skit he had been taught as a child to display his pride in his "edication."

After I went to college, My Daddy became a kind of hero for me. He gave me a telescoped view of my future as an "educated" black man and showed me how to become one.

MY DADDY, AN EDUCATIONAL ROLE MODEL

Combined, My Daddy and my mother had about a sixth-grade education, and my mother had most of that. Their rural Georgia elementary education was not as good as my Michigan elementary education, and my Michigan education did not prepare me for college.

Each evening, My Daddy struggled as he read aloud from his Bible. Each utterance rolled off his lips in a slow, deliberate, torturous cadence. He vocalized each word as though he were chewing rocks as he read.

He also often spoke what seemed to be a foreign language: "thee," "thou," "woe," and "ye." The biblical language was his idea of standard English. So when he read from my books, he pronounced "the" as "thee." We soon stopped reading near each other. I could neither read nor understand his Bible, and he could neither read nor understand my books.

For reasons unfathomed by me back then, by the time I was eight my parents were not able to help me much with my

Making a Way Out of No Way

homework. Even though I was eager to achieve in school, I soon discovered that my father and my mother could not help me. As I got older, I became aware that my mother was having baby after baby and was doing her homemaking chores by hand without any labor-saving devices. And by the time I had finished the first grade, I had as much formal school knowledge as my father.

Early on, I was naive and egoistic and resentful of My Daddy's not being able to tutor me. I felt deprived by his not giving me help with my homework. By the end of the third grade, not only could I read better than My Daddy could, but I could write better too, and I began to feel some false pride about my new formal education.

Despite his lack of formal schooling, in time My Daddy became an educational role model for me. As limited as their educations were, my parents taught me two very important values: how to learn and why to learn.

Through all of his stumbling and bumbling through his readings, My Daddy was still modeling for me that personal edification and educational betterment were essential. He also modeled for me that formal knowledge made individuals more capable of solving life's problems. Moreover, he showed me that those who could neither read nor write well had continuous trouble in their lives, especially in understanding what they were signing.

Notwithstanding my parents' lack of formal education and their inability to tutor me, I was promoted from 1A to 1B in the first grade.

My achieving a Ph.D. cannot be explained by the amount of tutorial help my parents gave me. My parents (particularly My Daddy) taught me something qualitatively different from formal educational skills and knowledge. My Daddy particularly modeled for me that extraordinary determination was required for effective learning. He modeled for me that struggle and perseverance day after day and night after night were required

JOSEPH W. SCOTT

for any serious acquisition of knowledge. And most important, he modeled for me that intelligence was acquired through hard work and was not an innate "gift."

HUSBAND/WIFE AND FAMILY RELATIONS

Whenever one of us boys failed to do our household chores, or whenever we showed any inkling of laziness, my mother used to say, "You'll never be the man yo fatha is." Being "smart" beyond our ages, we had figured out that My Daddy was uneducated, unsophisticated, and uncultured by middle-class standards, and we did not want to be like that anyway.

My Daddy was a master hammer man and a pretty good shoe cobbler. He took pride in living by the Divine Plan and being a Complete Man.

When he had to, My Daddy used to sew the whole evening long, stopping occasionally on winter evenings to put some wood and coal in the potbellied stove. He would sit next to the red-hot stove and mend his socks, coveralls, and longjohns.

He did not like doing "women's work," and he could have refused, but he didn't. He took considerable pride in being able "to do" for himself and his children, if necessary, whether my mother was incapacitated or not.

He expressed approval when my mother forced us boys to learn how to wash, iron, cook, sew, and feed and bathe babies. And he was glad when my mother could sit in a rocking chair and direct all of us through the household chores from there. Under her direction, we cooked the meals, washed the clothes, scrubbed the floors, and fed and bathed the younger children.

My Daddy wasn't as skilled as my mother, but he created the right rationales for us boys to feel okay about doing housework. He taught us by example that doing housework was more than a matter of pride and politics. It was about personal competency and self-sufficiency.

He used to say, "When you cain't do dese thangs for yoself,

23

womens will control you." He took pride in the fact that he was not like some of his peers who were dependent on their wives for cooked meals and clean and ironed clothes.

He told us that his workmates sometimes made their wives angry, and their wives would stop performing services for them, thereby coercing the men into conforming to their wishes. My Daddy's situation was different. "When yo mama stops doin' fo me, I don't pay her no mind, cause I can do fo myself."

From My Daddy, I learned that husband-wife relations were both emotional and political, and that knowledge of housework was power. I learned that husbands and wives played power games with housework, yardwork, and driving the car. I also learned that when either a husband or a wife knows how to perform tasks that the other cannot perform, the knowledgeable person has power over the other.

By his examples writ large, My Daddy taught me that personal competency is the wisest policy. Skills, knowledge, and conduct acquired in everyday life are sources of power and pride.

To this day I measure my personal autonomy by my personal competency.

BEING RIGHTEOUS

My Daddy used to quote the Bible to my mother about a wife's place. He used to tell Ma how it was a wife's place to obey her husband. He would say, "Wife, submit yourself unto your own husband, as unto the Lord." Ma would simply say in a calm voice, "But the husband's got to be righteous."

Money was always in short supply with ten children to provide for; so they often disagreed about the little money they had. They argued over how it was to be used: Was it to be used to pay on the gas bill ? the water bill? the grocery bill? the rent? Or what? And what about those little personal necessities like work gloves? Time after time as they argued about money, he'd say to my mother, "You call yourself a Christian? Well, the husband

JOSEPH W. SCOTT

is head of the wife, even as Christ is head of the church." But as always, Monda would say, "The husband's got to be righteous."

I do know when he started bringing home his check. By the time I became aware, My Daddy was already bringing home his paycheck without even cashing it and without taking out any money for personal things such as pipe tobacco or work gloves. My mother sent me to the store to cash his check and instructed me carefully to bring all of the money back to her. Coming from one of those Big Mamas, her words were so authoritative that they struck fear in my heart even as I thought about possibly bringing the money back to My Daddy.

After I brought the money home, Monda divided it for the bills. If there was any left over, she would give My Daddy some coins for either gloves or tobacco. Most of the time, it seemed, there was no money left after the bills were paid. My Daddy would look so sad and hurt at these times. But he didn't force his way. He would just start reading those same passages again and again, and quoting the Bible again and again. "The husband is head of the home, as Christ is head of the church."

My Daddy worked in the Chevrolet hammer shop in front of a huge fiery furnace spewing life-threatening heat. His job was to use a large pair of tongs and put in cold steel rods and turn them until they were red, then take them out and put them into a giant press for shaping. My Daddy needed rawhide gloves as much for the protection against the jagged steel as for the searing heat, but he did not always have a pair that completely covered his hands. On those days when he didn't have protection, he came home with bleeding fingers cracked wide open. Rather than ball up his fists and fight my mother, he'd just soak them in warm salty water, then read his Bible aloud.

Those were the times I felt most angry with my mother for not giving him money for gloves. I used to think that if I had ten children and worked as hard as he did to clothe, feed, and shelter them, I would cash my own check, take out the money I wanted, and then give the rest to my wife. I used to feel the anger My Daddy did not openly express.

Every morning before dawn, My Daddy prayed aloud, and again at the supper meal, and again at bedtime. He was a praying man, our religious leader. Sometimes, though, his patience wore thin, and he would question why only my mother decided how his check was to be spent. His anger would show, but he still would not use force to get his way. He would insist, however, that a wife is supposed to be subject to the will of her husband. But my mother was having none of that now that she was the chief cook, bottle washer, and money manager.

And so it was all of his working days while I was still at home. And during all of those years I used to think of My Daddy as weak. I used to tell myself that he was letting my mother boss him around.

After I became a father of three children under the age of five at the same time, I started to see him and his behavior differently. I believe with all my heart that he was just trying to be righteous, and the way of the righteous is pretty darn hard.

COMING TO SEE EYE TO EYE WITH MY DADDY

My Daddy dramatized in quite vivid terms that each nickel I earned would be "hard to come by." By the sheer force of his example, he taught me that it was going to take much more than hard work and self-denial to make a nickel or two. Just being black, in and of itself, was punishable as a crime in America.

When I could not eat or drink at the Holiday Inn in Georgia, or sleep in that or any other motel even with money with which to pay, it was then that I saw the world through My Daddy's eyes. When I walked a mile in his shoes in the same Georgia he had known as a child and young man and saw blacks get off the sidewalks for whites, and saw blacks drink at fountains labeled "colored," then My Daddy's reality became my reality. I truly could see eye to eye with My Daddy now.

JOSEPH W. SCOTT

But one night after attending an NAACP civil rights meeting and then going to bed, I awoke in the dark hours of the morning, then woke up my wife and infant children and led them outside because our house was on fire.

It was then that I understood My Daddy's admonition: "Boy, don't you know white folks will *kill* you."

Street Scene

JOHN McCLUSKEY, JR.

2. Harlem Montage: A Group Interview

The following interview took place late on the evening of July 14, 1990. It lasted more than three hours and ranged over a number of topics. The edited excerpts below remain in their original sequencing. Some cutting was done to reduce repetition.

Paul was the group coordinator, as it turned out. He knew the other four men from different contexts. He, Robert, and Patrick were recent converts to and members of New Hope Seventh-Day Adventist Church. They shared this information when the introductions were made. Paul had grown up in Valdosta, Georgia, where he met and befriended Fred, well before both moved separately to New York. Walter and Paul became close friends upon Paul's arrival in New York. Robert and Patrick were meeting Fred and Walter for the first time.

Three questions initiated the interview:

•What are the most immediate and long-range problems for African American males?

•What successful strategies can you identify that attempt to confront a specific problem?

•From your background, training, and experience, what do you think can be done about the problems of African American males?

VOICES

FRED: 54; reared in Detroit, Michigan, and Valdosta, Georgia; courier; divorced
PAUL: 49; reared in Valdosta, Georgia; former Army Honor Guard; manager of a New York City export firm; described himself as a "street hustler" at the time of the interview; divorced
PATRICK: 28; born in Costa Rica, reared in Brooklyn; employee at AT&T; single
ROBERT: "40 plus"; reared in New York City; married
WALTER: 53; born and reared in Jacksonville, Florida; BA, Florida A&M; accounting supervisor at a Bronx community mental health center; married

IDENTITY AND SELF-RESPECT

FRED: My present concern is the use, here on the East Coast, particularly in New York City, of the word "nigger" by the young teenagers and even younger. They have no idea what the word really means and no idea of the implications. It's become an awful situation because it's going from kindergarten even to the college level. It's really, really frightening culturally. I can see that it will create generations of disrespect, because when you lose your self-respect, then no one else has reason to respect you. I think the schools and everybody everywhere should encourage the fact that that is really a bad word, and there should be some kind of encouragement not to use it.

WALTER: One overriding general theme could really summarize the problem of the black man in a capsule, and that is an awareness of oneself. You've got to first find yourself from within. We could say that it's economics or it's this or that, but in a capsule it's the finding of one's self internally, and from that springs forth everything else. So it can't really be blamed, I don't think, on the white man, on women. You can't blame it on

JOHN MCCLUSKEY, JR.

finances, it can't be blamed on family. I think you have to really get down and find from within, from whence you cometh, and from that is where everything else springs forth. That's where the leadership comes from. Find yourself from within first, which most black men have not done. I profess that that's why a lot of them turn to the drug scene or to alcohol—thinking that you may find it within those external forces. But you'd never find it there; you've got to go deeper.

PAUL: I agree that one must know oneself. But I'm sure that some of the problems that our mothers and our children and even ourselves are in happen because we don't know ourselves. We're the only people who can't write home. We can't receive letters from home because we know nothing about where we come from. And by not knowing where you come from, how can you know where you're going? We must have a sense of family, a sense of values for an individual self. Even the Jews had a family structure while they were enslaved. Even today they still have a sense of belonging. We don't know what happened twenty years ago. We have the same problem [with racism] all over, not just here in America. I think knowledge of self is important, but I see a greater enemy. I can blame almost everything on the systematic effort by white people to keep black people down. Thank you.

PATRICK: I can understand the point that has been made, but personally I feel that the black man has been branded all over the world. It doesn't matter where he goes, he just seems to get a bad rap. Looking at it from an economic or social or spiritual point of view, me not being born in this country and having relatives that are not from this country, I get to see both sides. In Central America the black man is a little more confident despite the lack of everything else they have there. That's because it all boils down to the family. It's true that we have to look at our past, but we just can't look at our past all of the time. White people have done a lot of things wrong, but blacks were no angels either. We

31

need to start looking ahead and start really feeling at peace with ourselves, more content, and just take it from that point.

ROBERT: I feel that today there is no "solution" to this problem. We talk about it, and there isn't going to be any solution if you have even two white men on this earth. I remember my mother used to always say, "As long as there are two men on this earth, there's going to be a problem." And it's proven true. I can go back to when it was Cain and Abel—two men that were brothers, they were equal in everything, but one had more of a worship for God than the other, and there was a problem there. And we're always going to have a problem. But with the black man now, he's had a bigger problem. Paul said something about how the black man was brought over here. But the way I look at it, sure we were brought over here in slavery, but it was all done for a reason. And I say this because I'm deep into Bible study, into Christ, period. The way I see it, God lets things happen for a reason. There's a reason why we're here. There's a reason why all of these problems are going on, but it's not only the black man that's being hit hard; other men have been hit hard, too. We have a drug situation here where I hear folks say the white man has the black man fighting against the black man, fighting himself for the territory. But in solving the problem, I mean, with Christ, it's an endless hope. Without Christ is a hopeless end. . . . They have this commercial out now where this deacon wants every station to play against racial harmony. No matter what you do, you know you can't make people like people. I don't care who they are—Italian, Jew, Greek, Puerto Rican. You just can't make people like people. Likeness comes from Christ, with Christ within so that you can bring this likeness out.

FRED: Gentlemen, racism in America is an institution. It's the second oldest institution in America, and don't you ever forget it. It starts with the church. It starts with the Catholics and the Protestants. We've had more holy wars than any other kind of wars known to men. Like Robert said, differences of opinion,

JOHN MCCLUSKEY, JR.

my wanting to be right, what's to make you wrong? Because I legislated in my own mind, not that it has to be right. For instance, do you know how the white man gets away with the idea that he can inflict slavery on us and treat us so wrongly in a pay scale in the work market? Because he picks up the Bible—and I can't tell you what chapter or verse—but we're supposed to be the children of Ham, and you know what it says? It says the children of Ham will draw the water from the well. In other words, we will be the servants. But the Bible is like anything else: you can take it and use it any way you want. I have to agree with Paul. The institution of racism is 95 percent of our trouble because we have been under it for all our lives.

WALTER: Hold it, Freddie . . .

FRED: You've got it, Mr. Walter. I'm finished with it now. I just want to remind you of what I felt about it and what I know about it.

WALTER: See my whole point is, I'm not going to allow you to use racism as an excuse because that's what a lot of people are doing—using it as an excuse to sit back on their behinds and do nothing and blame the white man for all their troubles, their miseries, and their sorrows. No, I'm not letting you off the hook that easy. There's some type of racism or religious discontent all over the world. The only one that can hold you back is you. Can't no white man hold you back; he can hold you back if you want to use that as the excuse. It's too simple to say that it's all racism—that 95 percent of our problem is racism.

FRED: Yes, it is—95 percent of our problem is racism.

WALTER: 95 percent of our problem may be *thinking* it's racism.

FRED: 95 percent of our problem is racism.

WALTER: 95 percent of the problem is not racism.

Harlem Montage

FRED: Walter, Walter, there are so many doors that are closed to us that will never be opened.

WALTER: Yeah, as long as you sit back and say that the white man got the door closed so that you can't open it. Boy, I haven't seen a door yet that couldn't be kicked in.

FRED: Walter, Walter, we haven't been out of slavery two hundred years yet. I think we've made amazing progress. We still have generations of humpty-dumpt that's got to go down. I think it's going to take us another five hundred years before we really have ourselves together. I think the next five hundred years being black will be a wonderful thing, but right now it's really rough, man, because we just got out of the shed.

ECONOMICS AND EDUCATION

J. Mc.: It seems that the conflict we're having is whether the main problem is institutional racism or one's sense of self. And the two could in fact flow together, but let's see if we can pin it down to institutions first. For example, we may talk about family at some point, but suppose that your particular belief in God is shaped around a particular church, and another particular view is shaped around a different church. I'm trying to figure out a way that we can come together despite the differences in religious backgrounds. So suppose we all join forces in the community to deal with the educational system. What could we agree upon that would deal with the youth in our community? What kinds of things can we agree upon that should go on in the school system that are not going on in the school system?

PAUL: Speaking personally, we don't have all of these things interconnected. And with family and knowing of the self and everything, each of us usually has some kind of family behind us, some kind of situation. Right now in a lot of states the government has allotted a certain amount of money for a school depending on the tax base that this particular neighborhood and

34

people enjoy. If you lived in Beverly Hills with a high tax base, then more money would be going to education. If you lived in Watts, Harlem, less money would be allotted. Now you take the situation in Illinois, where the whole city is bankrupt and they had an earthquake. What part of Illinois was that—East St. Louis? The whole system is bankrupt because all of the businesses have left and they have allotted the money to the outskirts of town. These are the people enjoying perfect education. They can't even pick up the garbage in this area. So it's all institutionalized racism.

Now our particular case here, even in Harlem there are different people coming over to this country, and they have their needs and their wants, and they're not even hiring black people. Japanese recently began owning all kinds of places. They [African Americans] find out the Japanese don't want to have nothing to do with them. The employment agency was told not to even send them. And you've got people that's coming over to this country with the downing of the Berlin Wall. You're going to have all kinds of people looking for remedial jobs just like black people are having to do now. Right now in Harlem we have four average stores on each corner, and not one black child working there. Do you know what it would mean for one black family, for one person in the family, to be there to work? They've got a different idea altogether for it. Meanwhile we have churches going up. I really believe our situation is economic.

But usually when a person gets an education, they move out of the neighborhood, and then who do the children have to look up to? They see me, old Paul with his hat drooped to the side, with some girl riding in the car who looks like she's a white woman. That is the only thing that they've got to look at. They don't have nobody walking around with a briefcase, and they can't even get a job. Believe it or not, in Harlem it was easier for me to get an education than it is for a kid nowadays with all the disruptions in school. And at least if a person wanted to go to school, they could get a part-time job, picking up bottles or sweeping up. Nowadays they can't even get a part-time job. So

35

what do our kids do? They go sell crack. They can buy a $25 piece of cocaine, mix it up, put it together, and sell $100 worth of crack, or $200 if they really want to make it garbage, and that's all that they're doing. And if they can keep $10 over here, $10 over there, then pretty soon you'll see one of them driving a car, a Jeep or something like that. Even myself right now, if I was coming up—say I wanted an education or something—I might be tempted by that; it's the only job really paying something. I thought education was supposed to help black men. It helped white women with equal rights for women. It helped all the other people that came to this country, and the black man still finds himself on the lonely island, just like Martin Luther King, there by himself. People should just boycott these companies. That's what Gandhi did. Gandhi walked three thousand miles to get salt before he would pay taxes on British salt.

J. Mc.: That's an excellent point in terms of economic boycotts. How would you connect that to schools? This sounds like a problem that takes place outside the boundaries of school.

PAUL: Well, economics is part of education anyway. Most colleges are priced out of most black people's reach, first of all. There are little foundations that really help them, but the government is cutting back on everything. I was telling you recently about whites protesting affirmative action programs, so it's a never-ending battle for black people. And without education you can't go nowhere.

BLACK-ON-BLACK CRIME

WALTER: I was saying that the majority of violent crimes against blacks are perpetrated by blacks. I witnessed one myself. An old black lady was coming down the street. This young black dude had on sneakers, ran up to her, knocked her down, and stomped her. She had blood on the side of her head. I was watching from the other side of the street. He grabbed her

JOHN MCCLUSKEY, JR.

pocketbook, took off and ran. Now, how does this racism that you're talking about, that people have done to us, relate to incidents like that?

PAUL: Lack of knowledge of self.

WALTER: So that's not racism, then. So what we're really saying . . .

FRED: Wait a minute. Racism comes from that same social family that we were talking about.

WALTER: Okay, so he grabbed the old lady, beat her, threw her down, because the white man didn't give his mother and father the proper opportunity to go to school, to teach him so that he wouldn't do that.

FRED: Yeah, that's about it.

WALTER: That's stretching it very far.

FRED: Yeah, we've been stretching it for four hundred years. . . .

J. Mc.: Along those same lines, let's connect that brother's position to education. Could you conceive of anything in the institution of education that can give him a stronger sense of self? What kinds of things could go on, at least in the schools, to help deal with the sense of self?

WALTER: The only thing wrong with education is the system—the whole American system itself. The problem is that the school does not really have control over the youth. There was a time when I think they had more control than they have now. Under the system in which most of us came up, teachers had control, and they were able to teach kids. Now it's very difficult to teach kids because the system has put in all of these rules and regulations that give the advantage to the child. You can't touch him. In fact, the child is almost allowed to do anything he wants. Also, you used to have to pass him; our kids have been finishing

Harlem Montage

high school without even having learned the courses. Secondly, the schools are mandated to accept anybody that comes, any kids; if they stay out for two or three months and then come back, you've got to let them in. And the other thing is that one bad kid can really disrupt the whole class—nobody can learn anything. Even if there are thirty kids in that class, twenty-nine want to learn and one doesn't want to learn, there's nothing that you can do about that one. You can't put him out on the street. You see, what we're really talking about is a much higher thing than that. We're talking about the total Constitution and all the freedoms that they allow one to have, even the criminal justice system. It takes a lot to send a person to jail. The freedom that a person enjoys a lot of times can be a detriment to him. Kids don't have to go to school if they don't want to. You can't make them go.

ROBERT: We talked about education, and we talked about the children, but what about the parents? Aren't they responsible to see that their children get the best education and to be sure that they go to school and that they have some type of Jesus in between their ears to have their fear of God, respect for God, respect for father, respect for mother, so they don't knock down some lady and stomp her? Shouldn't it start in the home with the parents?

FRED: You know what the Bible says about training a child? Train a child in the womb in the way that it should go. My mama showed me that in the Bible because I was telling her that when I grew up I was going to get married and make her a grandma. And she said, "You don't know what you're talking about, son; let me show you something. When I carried you, I did a lot of reading, I did my exercises, I tried to have you as normal and alert a child as I could possibly have."

ROBERT: But eating the right foods and all of that is also in the womb between mother and father. Even before conception this thing is carried on. Because you don't just have a child and

JOHN MCCLUSKEY, JR.

that's it. It is done male or female before; that's the way training of a child begins. I agree with you on that 100 percent.

PATRICK: Someone brought up that the majority of everyone here came up in the old school, where it was a different setting than what it is today. I think what our parents went through, coming up in such a bad society, gave us strength to strive harder. And you would see the fruits of your parents and certain blacks in top positions today. Not all blacks are really bad; I mean, there are some blacks that have reached certain levels that we all have aspirations to achieve. So we have to give them credit too. But what can we do about the school problem? I agree that it goes back a little before school; you've got to have a certain kind of atmosphere in the home. The nucleus, the family, that's where it all starts, because from birth all the way up to age seven, that's the most devastating impression that the mind can take at one time, and from that point you take it all the rest of your life. That's going to affect you even when you're seventy-five years old. So the first seven years are really important, and I think there should be a lot less time in front of the TV and a lot less time in front of other outside influences, because media plays a very important role. You take that away and instead you push values in that place—the same values that you grew up with, the basics.

Also, I think schools should go a little further in what they teach as far as technical or academics. And when I say that, I mean how to have more moral values for your fellow man. You want to see a change? Put that into the school system and you'll see a big difference. How to treat one another better. You don't want to see anyone hurting your sister, someone that's born within your family, but imagine if you treated all women as you treat her. Also how to function within society, how to get along after three o'clock, after the bell rings or after school gets out. Sure, teachers show how to deal with certain situations, economically, politically, and socially, as far as what the school tells us, but sometimes it's not enough, and that's where stress comes in. You can have all of these things, and they all have their place in life, but it would mean nothing without Christ in your life. Christ puts everything back together again. And that's the same value that your parents had and their parents had because of the hard times that they had; they needed something to look up to. Everybody, it doesn't matter where you come from, people may say that they're atheist or something, but every man that has been born knows that there's something higher than themselves.

J. Mc.: So you would allow not only Christians, but the Muslims and Hindus; you would say exactly what you said just now but also be able to apply that to Mohammed and to other religions—that there is that higher being that you would be able to live with, and in school . . .

PATRICK: I'm not too much to promote religion in school because that seems to cause a controversy, but what I'm saying is moral values.

WALTER: You mean religious values?

PATRICK: No, we were talking about the school system and I didn't say religious values, I said moral values.

WALTER: But you said Christ is the one that ties it all together.

PAUL: Yeah, but I said that starts in the home.

WALTER: But what about Buddha? Can he tie it all together?

PATRICK: No.

WALTER: Can Mohammed tie it all together? Can Moses?

PATRICK: No.

WALTER: So only Christ can tie it all together?

PATRICK: Can I ask you a question? The Bible says that there's only one name . . .

JOHN MCCLUSKEY, JR.

WALTER: No, I'm not asking you what your Bible says . . .

PATRICK: Christ is the answer.

PAUL: Robert said something about shouldn't moral values be taught in the home, and I'm sure that all of us would agree that it should be. Our children are learning a lot of the things that they do learn in school because that is the only source that they've got. Now, remember, I accepted Jesus as my savior, but I think the situation is so critical now that I would be ready to accept blacks with any supervision of their children, whether they're Buddhist or Hindu, and let them be exposed to all of it, and whatever come out let it come out—we would still have a better-structured society. For the sake of our children, we should get something together just because we're black people that can't even write a letter home. We should get together as far as school, economics, and everything else. My idea is to have an organization, but I don't know how Christ would want it. It's called BEEF, the Black Education and Economic Force, and that's what I want to do with my life. I would like to incorporate everybody into it that moves to America, cause this is a terrible thing that they are doing to our children. And do you know how much money is spent here in Harlem and how much money is being spent elsewhere, and everybody taking full advantage of it? If we could incorporate all of that money, we could use it, and we've got to teach our own children too. We can't have other people teaching our children so much, especially at a tender age.

FRED: Like he said, one through seven are the formative years.

PAUL: We've got to do something to come together with the Muslims. I would be willing to do that—I would be willing just to see the instruction, the well-structured organization where the money is coming in.

WALTER: Yeah, but that was his whole point—it can't be that way; you cannot be willing to back off Christ

PAUL: For the economic reason and for the education and for political reasons.

PATRICK: Even if someone fell into the category of Buddhism or some other religion, I think it would help them as far as some kind of discipline in school. Now back to what Paul said: you can't leave your kids unattended and then go out and do your thing, and when they go to school, expect the teachers to straighten out whatever problem could've been straightened out at home. No, it doesn't start there, it starts at home.

ROBERT: But what about those parents that leave their children unattended, and what do we have today, we have babies having babies. How are we going to get this education system up when the babies haven't even finished school? I don't know about in your neighborhood, but in mine I see these young girls every summer. I see a fresh bloom coming out, and these are young girls, fourteen and fifteen years old. Babies having babies. So to me education has to start in the home.

J. Mc.: Okay, it needs to start in the home, I would agree with that. That may happen, and we may all live to see that happen, but right now it's not happening.

WALTER: It may be impossible for it to happen in the home. You know why? Because you can't train kids if you were not trained yourself or if you have no values yourself. And in many homes, the mother and the father don't have any values to share with the kids.

FRED: But there are some that succeed.

WALTER: You mean there are some kids that succeed irrespective of the fact that their parents didn't teach them any [positive values]?

ROBERT: No, no, no, no—I'm talking about those that have

JOHN MCCLUSKEY, JR.

the values. They go back to Bible training, education and all that. Their children have come up and they have made names in this society.

WALTER: You mean some parents that didn't were misguided themselves, and so were their kids.

J. Mc.: I think we ought to make it a little more specific. Suppose that 80 percent are positive—those parents did a good job—and 20 percent are represented by the man who knocked down the older woman and kicked her and took her purse. What responsibility do we have outside of the family to deal with the other 20 percent? Is there anything in terms of education or religion to deal with that? Let's assume that the majority are doing a good job, but it's the minority that the fabric of the community may be threatened by. How do you begin to break that cycle? Is it enough to say that it's the fault of those parents for not teaching their children moral lessons?

WALTER: As far as us collectively as a group trying to deal with that other 20 percent, that goes back to what I said about the system. You can only deal with the 20 percent if they allow you to. In my day, if I was caught doing something across town, any adult—didn't have to get no permission—would beat my butt, and then if he saw my mother in church, he would tell her and I would get another one.

PAUL: Would you let someone do your child like that today?

WALTER: Today the system is different. Then the community took care of its own, and my mother and father would have thanked her for beating my behind—and given me another on top of it. Today, you had better not go over to that child and chastise him. You can't interject yourself into that situation. There's going to be more problems for you. When the child goes home and tells his parents that you bothered with him, they're going to come after you and call you a child molester. So the 80 percent has to be very careful about trying to deal personally with the 20 percent.

That is why the 80 percent has to set up a vehicle or an avenue where they're not directly involved. That's supposed to be what community centers, afterschool activities, trips for the disadvantaged are for. That's supposed to be what our tax money is going for, for summer jobs so youth will have something to do and won't get into trouble. That's what probation officers are supposed to be for. No, nowadays the 80 percent, because of the system, can't directly interject themselves into a solving of that problem, except through their representatives.

PATRICK: I think it can be done. It starts like you said, with the community, outside of the home. Of course, you've got your block association, you're taking care of your neighbor's children, and all these other activities that are going on. But it's going to take a longer time for us because it seems like we have been warped in our way of thinking. We have opened our minds to let a lot of things in.

PAUL: Black people are going to have to realize that we don't have any others but ourselves, and we've got to come to the understanding that we've got to solve our problems. In my own division, BEEF, I don't want no white person making no decisions. I don't even want one in it.

WALTER: So, you see, it's the color that bothers you?

FRED: It's the color. He don't have to live within the decision.

PAUL: Wait a minute. The Jewish organizations have Jews in them, Polish people have Polish, Italians have Italians. Why can't black people have a group? What's the problem?

PATRICK: The only reason Jewish people are banding together right now is because they have a common ground.

JOHN MCCLUSKEY, JR.

PAUL: Don't we?

PATRICK: I'm not taking anything away from that. I'm just saying that if Jewish people were the only ones on earth, they'd have a little discrimination within their own group, too. It's not going to stop there.

PAUL: We're not talking about what they would do. I'm not talking about anything hypothetical. I'm talking about what we're facing now. I wouldn't have them in it because they don't qualify to be in the organization. When you have a family, you have a family discussion—I'm not supposed to be in the discussion.

WALTER: So you're talking about reverse racism?

PAUL: How can I be racist when I'm the victim?

WALTER: You don't want them even coming to your neighborhood.

PAUL: If it's not a matter of racism, it's a matter of that we could help by getting together. Do you know what heritage is? It is people who experienced common ground, common behavior, common ancestry. So these people that have something in common should be the ones that do it, and nobody should try to talk them out of it. If rich and poor come together we could solve this, and we would have a dramatic front.

PATRICK: That's one thing that man has not solved. So many accomplishments, and racism is one thing that you can't solve.

INSTITUTIONS

J. Mc.: In addition to religion, what do you find to be the most important factors, elements, and episodes in your life that helped shaped your thinking as an African American male? I know everybody could come up with about twenty things that are important to shaping who they are. Maybe we can call them turning points.

FRED: Well, gentlemen, to let the cat out of the bag—I'm a racist. [*general laughter*] When I was six years old, my mother sent me to the store to get some Brazil nuts. An old cracker asked me what I wanted, and I told him some Brazil nuts like my mama had told me, and he said, "Oh, you want some nigger toes." I didn't know nothing like that, so I went back and told Mama. She carried me back to the store and said, "You tell him what you want, Fred." The cracker repeated himself. She said, "Come on out here, son," and we didn't buy them. The way he sneered and went on to my mother, I wanted to kill him. And then I got a dislike for all white people. I used to say I wished I knew when I was going to die, and I'd spend my whole day killing every one of them I could. I grew up with that in me and I've never liked them, and probably never will.

ROBERT: It is only Christ that can change your heart. Cause he that hateth his brother is a murderer. I know you must have a concept that when you die you are either going to a heaven or a hell. Nobody wants to go to a hell; they want to go to heaven, they want peace forever and all that. All that hatred has to come out of your heart. My brother, it's only Christ that can change your heart on that matter there, that racism. My advice to you is to seek him out and get him to change your heart—no matter what your problem is, he can change it.

J. Mc.: Fred dug way back into his childhood to an incident that really shaped him. Robert, was there a positive love-harmony model that you were aware of early on?

ROBERT: I was shopping around at religions—Muslims, Catholics, Episcopalian, Baptist, Methodist—but none of them hit me one way or the other. I was more or less raised in an Adventists' church, but I went to other different religions as well. But in 1981 I went to a tent on 135th Street, and the man was preaching at me there, and I'll tell you this—it is only the

46

Holy Spirit that guides you and leads you into a situation of bringing one to oneself. When I heard this man speaking, it brought back what I had heard a long time ago in the Adventist message, and somehow the spirit of the Lord was telling me it was right, this was the right thing, because it was Christ, it's Jesus Christ. Without Christ you can't do nothing. I heard he was coming back to me, then things began to change, and I found myself after six weeks of listening. I got baptized and that's it. So it's Christ now, and by the grace of God, Christ forevermore. I can't see myself changing or going back, knowing what I know now. And it's a continual learning because you can read John 3:16 fifteen thousand times, and you'll get a different application out of it every time. And that goes for the rest of the Bible: you read it, you get a different application every time, and it applies to your soul's salvation.

J. Mc.: Let's get back to the question of the most significant thing in your background that helped shape your self-concept as an African American male.

WALTER: I think the most dominant thing that affected my ideas as an African American was joining an all-black fraternity. At the time they had very high standards to get in there, and you wouldn't believe the concepts, ideas, and attitudes that I learned, going across the burning sand with them. First of all, being totally confident in yourself as a black male. Some of the rituals involved self-control, which a lot of black men don't have. Being able to control your emotions, any time that you want—for example, having to stand there and let someone slap you. Ordinary people would hit back and fight. I did too, the first time, and he said, "You should only get mad whenever you want to get mad. You cannot allow other people to dictate how you're going to be." We would have classes and sessions on it. Eventually I learned that I can get angry when I want to, or don't want to. It's not up to anyone else that's going to make me be a particular way.

Then we went on to having confidence in your fellow black

47

brother. I'll never forget one thing that was so impressive: we were all standing around, and they took a big stone and tied a string onto it, then tied the string around my private parts and stood me on a table. I had the stone in my hand, and the string was tied around here [*indicates scrotum*], and I was looking out at my black brothers. They said, "Okay, Walter, the stone is heavy, right? Walter, we want you to drop the stone." I said, "No, I can't do this." They said that they were brothers. "You've got to trust us. All for one and one for all. If you can't deal with watching, we'll put the blindfold on you." So I put the blindfold on, and they told me again to drop it. I dropped it—bam—and nothing happened. While I was putting the blindfold on, they had detached the string from the stone. I dropped it and I said "ooooohhhhhh," and then we all gathered around and cried together. The lesson was you've got to trust your brothers. We're all brothers under the sun.

GROUP: That was good. [*general nods of agreement and low-fives all around*]

PAUL: There are so many things that shape a person's life. The army had a devastating effect on me from a good point, discipline. That's where I learned that there were different ways to fight. To solve my problem before that, I always believed that if somebody did something to me, I'd punch them out. But I found out that there's other ways to beat people. Like the white boys—just assassinate their character, their good name; tell a lie on them to accuse them of something that they didn't want, just to put them down. If you punched one of them in the mouth, you were in bigger trouble. I had to find a new way to fight.

I remember one time a guy told us that we could have a three-day pass if we cut down the grass in a field that was as tall as I was. I only had four men, and I was in charge of this detail. We were about ten miles into the woods, and they sent somebody back for us at four o'clock. Otherwise we were supposed to walk back. We wanted this pass so bad, and we were chanting like a

JOHN MCCLUSKEY, JR.

chain gang, singing. And when they came back for us, we weren't quite finished—we had a little bit left. The guy said, "I know you all want your pass, but what about me? I ain't going nowhere. I just came to pick you up. If you aren't coming now, I'm going on back." We told him to go ahead cause we wanted this pass. We walked however many miles afterwards about five o'clock, and chow was already over. All I was looking to do was hit the showers and get on the bus to go back to New York.

When I got back there, this cracker told me, "Thomas, you're going to stand an inspection." Now, everybody knew they were going to have an inspection, and everyone else got off at twelve o'clock to stand up and clean their utensils and make their beds. I've been out since six o'clock in the morning. The other guys in the platoon were gone, so I went in there and tried to wash these things and clean them, but at nine o'clock I still wasn't finished. I knew I wanted to do something to this boy, very very bad. He made me stand this inspection. Mentally I couldn't take it anymore. I said, "I'm going," and I kicked all the stuff off the bed. The first sergeant grabbed me and said, "Paul, what's wrong?" He came in the army the same time that I did, and he treated me like this. I said, "I respect you because you can take it and this little ol'"—I had a name for him—"he wouldn't even speak to me on the sidewalk." Anyway, he told me to go on home; he knew how hard I worked. I left about eleven o'clock and got home by twelve, but I still was out of there. But to be put through that—I would rather have them punch me. So I found other ways to hurt people, where before then I knew of only one alternative of hurting a person—physically hurting them. So this is one thing that I've learned in my life. There have been other things, such as girls and church, but that was one thing that made me know how to fight. Now I see politicians and how they can wreck someone's career and assassinate a person's character, call them everything but a child of God. And that leads me to the point about black people. They have been always scandalized, believing something less than everything that has to do with them. That's why we hate each other. That's why we cut each other. That's why they took the old lady, because everybody else can do something. We're the only ones—we've got to strike out at somebody.

PATRICK: I can identify with what Paul was saying. In '79 I graduated from high school and joined the army. I didn't know what I wanted to do with myself. All I knew was that I wanted to try something else other than New York. When I went in, I didn't realize what I was doing, because I was totally giving up my freedom. I could say the army had its way with me, but as Paul said, it taught you how to fight other than being physical, especially coming from a physical environment. I came in as a sub-level, starting right from the bottom, up to rank as an E-6 in five years. I had a four-by-two contract, which meant four years active and two in reserve. I met a lot of prejudice, not just because I was black but because I was from New York also. There were just so many things that I wasn't used to, and it made me very, very angry and upset. I was very upset that I handed over my freedom to these people and on a contract.

I decided to fight fire with fire, and I made up my mind that the best way for me to get out of it was to be an officer. So I went to officers' candidate school, and I was degraded, humiliated to do certain things. It's not worth it, but at the time it's drilled so much in your head that this is what you believe. I did everything that I set out to do, but at the very end, at graduation, the commandants' captain did something real dirty to me. He went back to my records from when I first came in—I had brought some of my bad habits into the army, and I was selling drugs and had gotten caught. He knew it all along and he let me go all the way through it, and then at graduation he snatched me out. This was right before the pinning of the medal on the collar. To satisfy me, he gave me a certificate that said that I completed officers' candidate school, but of course I got no merit for it with the federal government. I was really very, very upset. I didn't care

JOHN MCCLUSKEY, JR.

about discharge or AWOL, so I just left. If they wanted to come after me, they could. My sergeant found out what had happened to me, and he sympathized and stopped certain procedures from going after me. I have the experience of being in the military, and it taught me how to deal with people, but it also taught me always to be in control of my own self, to make my own destiny, so to speak. Of course that's what I thought before I became a Christian. I know a lot better now, but even you can't control your own destiny without Christ. That was a bad experience that stuck with me for a very long time, and I was very irate about the situation.

J. Mc.: I think everybody agrees how important family is, especially in the early years. And when we think of the family, we think of at least two roles, a male role and a female role—a mother role, a father role; for some reason sometimes a father has to take over the mother role, or the mother has to take over the father role. All of us here are fathers or about to be fathers, or will someday be fathers. We learn our lesson of fatherhood from fathers or father figures, often someone we were close to. I'd like you to search your memory. I'm not going to ask what was the most important lesson that you learned from your father, but what are some of the things that stuck out in your experience with your father that you've tried to apply in your own position?

WALTER: My father came up with a different system than what we are used to now, and he died at a relatively young age. But I'll tell you what I remember about him: he was a good provider. He got me to work with him during the summertime; he had his boss hire me when I was in junior and senior high school. He was a sewer worker. Did you ever see that show *The Honeymooners* with Ralph Kramden and Norton? Well, he had Norton's job, for the city of Jacksonville—he would go down in the sewer and clean them out. So I worked alongside him there. And of course we had to ride on the back of the truck; we weren't allowed to sit in the seats. We always had to hop on the back and go out whether it was raining or not. Blacks were not allowed to ride in the cab.

There wasn't enough money for them to send me away to school, so I was able to get a scholarship. I was sitting in class one day, a sociology class, and someone said that I had a phone call. I went to the phone, and they told me that my father was dead. At the time I was nineteen, and nineteen is a relatively young age to lose your father. He had died of a heart attack, prostrate down in the sewer. Things like that kind of stick with you. I remember him as a loving, providing father. Of course he would drink liquor on the weekends and all, because most black men would do that, but on Monday morning he would go back to work again. Being that his life was snuffed out at such a young age, he and I weren't really able to communicate on past the age of nineteen. At the time, he was thirty-nine.

[*long pause*]

PATRICK: Me being the youngest out of everyone here, I don't have to dig too far back. [*laughter*] But I have to say one thing: I learned some good things from my father. My father received his education in Costa Rica under the English system, which is from Great Britain. So he had an English education and a Spanish education. He was a civil engineer. I can't remember what age he was then, he must have been about twenty-five. And in Costa Rica that was a big thing. He even worked with the U.S. Army in Panama as a civilian employee, next to the Panama Canal Zone. After that job, he left Costa Rica and did island hopping—Jamaica, Barbados, Trinidad, the American and British Virgin Islands. He went a little bit of everywhere and he did little jobs everywhere, and he finally made it here. He made it to Brunswick, New Jersey, in 1964 or '66, and then he sent for his family to come over.

He had several jobs when he came here, but he had never really experienced the prejudice that he experienced here, and that was a big thing for him because he couldn't really deal with

JOHN MCCLUSKEY, JR.

it. He couldn't understand it, so he decided that his family was not going to take this kind of prejudice. Number one, he spoke Spanish; number two, he's blacker than I am. That's two strikes against him. He sent us to school and tried to get into our heads the English system and tried to get rid of the Spanish. He also had said that if he could help it, his family wouldn't have to go through the prejudice that he did. He became an independent businessman: he made his own money, he had his own business, and ever since that time he has had his own contracting company. That's what I remember about my father—he never depended on people, but he depended on himself to generate money for his family. And if I learn anything from my father, it is to be self-sufficient, being independently in control of myself. I've always had it to employ myself, I'll always have that. And when you have your own company you can buy land, so I have to take that from my father. We didn't come up in a warm house—when I say warm house, I mean that he didn't have that much affection that he showed the children—but he was a good provider, a dedicated person.

FRED: My father and mother separated when I was between ten and eleven. We were living in Detroit, Michigan, and he was in the army. In 1946 we moved to Georgia, where my mother came from. We were there only a year, and my old man met another lady. They split up. But I remember my dad teaching me how to draw, how to use a slide rule. My old man was a handsome guy, and he was always spoiled by women. They were always at the man. I remember one of the most humiliating things in my life. I hit on a young chick when I was a teenager, and she said, "I don't want you, I want your daddy." I often wished that I had my dad's personality. I never seen him in an argument with another man, and I never seen any man that didn't like him. I can understand how my man went off cause my mother was always industrious. She'd be doing hair from nine in the morning till ten at night. That's how I learned how to cook and take care of myself. He just got involved with women. He too should be in his sixties, but he too died of a heart attack, same as his father did. Men in my family—heredity—die in their sleep a lot. My mother was very angry with that man for a very long time, and I suffered quite a bit of abuse for it. She never denied me anything because my mother is a very vain person; she would never have nobody say she didn't take care of her child. I had everything. I didn't know about poverty or nothing else, and it spoiled me. I've never been a serious enough person—I've had too much too easy, and I'm irresponsible at fifty-four years old right now.

PAUL: The best thing my father ever taught me, and I didn't like it at the time, was how to clean up the place. He always had some type of a business, and he would pay people more money than he would pay me for the same work. He said, "Hey, I'm taking care of you at home." And if I had one single thing left on the floor, he would make me sweep that whole floor over. I would say, "I could just go and pick that up, Daddy," and he said, "You've got to do it right if you're going to do it." Now I'm trying to teach my sons the same thing, cause you know if a person starts half-stepping in little things like that, then they'll go through life half-stepping. And everything that they do they won't apply themselves fully. Half-stepping is contagious. When you do something, you have to do it right, he taught me that.

The interview ended at 1:30 A.M. with the group agreeing that there was still much to talk about. I was leaving the city later the same morning, so I agreed to interview each separately by phone during the next week. The subject: women in their lives. Following are excerpts from those conversations.

PAUL

PAUL: As far as I'm concerned, women have bore the brunt of the burden when it comes to raising a family. Like I said before,

JOHN MCCLUSKEY, JR.

the white man mastered the black male. As a matter of fact, they castrated him completely. They didn't even want him to have bass in his voice. They didn't even want him to look the white man in the eye. However, the black woman historically raised the white children and was just as much a part of their upbringing. The black woman exerted a great influence as far as the white man is concerned and as far as the black man is concerned, as far as bringing up the children, even when it came to bringing home the bacon. The word "husband" means hus*band*. He is the one who is supposed to bind the family together, to keep them together. But the band that kept most black families together was always the woman. I would say some of them soon disrespected the males and utilized their newfound position as the sole provider. I guess they had reason to disrespect the male because some of the men were shiftless and lazy due to the constant overtones coming from higher up that the black man could never be a man, no way. If you would even try to chastise a woman, the police would lock you up. The black woman knew that. She always knew where she stood. And there's been a lot of documentation where a black man was taken to jail out of his own house—when he was just trying to be a hus*band* and a father in his house because the black women, some of them, have overstepped their authority.

J. Mc.: Anything directly personal you want to touch on?

PAUL: As far as my personal situation, I've had so many problems—especially my wife, the one who isn't exactly a virgin and now she's doing time. It's hard for me to rationalize her being promiscuous because I knew she was crazy about me and didn't want to give up that thing for me. And now it seems to me that it ain't nothing. There ain't no telling how many she done laid with and played with. It doesn't bother me anymore, but in time it just goes to show you how people can be changed. She didn't want nobody to hardly touch her in the beginning, and now she's in for robbery. I married somebody I couldn't predict. Every woman has disappointed me to some extent. That may

55

be one of the reasons I turned to God. He might not come when I want, but He's never late.

J. Mc.: You've piqued my curiosity. You're in a long relationship now that seems to be working.

PAUL: I've been with Juanita longer than I was with my mother, because when I was fifteen or sixteen they [mother and sisters] left. I learned to expect certain things. They say the longer a man don't have no woman, he don't have no problem, or if he hasn't had no problem with a woman, he hasn't had no woman. You get to a point in life where you say, "Well, where do I go from here? I know what this is. I know what's on the outside." Sometimes you stick with it, you make the best out of it. There are a lot of people that do that, but I'm not saying I'm completely dissatisfied or nothing like that. She can be changed and I can, too. After fifteen years, there are some things that I can depend on her for. And she knows that she can depend on me. She's had operations and there was nobody here to look after her but me. They all come to me when they have problems, you know— grandnieces that I look after, and everybody seems to have quite a respect for me. If something would happen to them, they'd call me and I'd have to get them out of all kinds of trouble. I'm more or less held in high regard. Maybe they're playing me like a guitar. I don't want to let them down either.

WALTER

WALTER: The Afro-American woman has played an important part in shaping the ideas and attitudes of the black male. I think it starts at the very beginning, when the male is born—he sees his mother and the ideas, attitudes, and all that she has. I think part of the black man's problem has been his ideas and attitudes about women. I think, though, a lot of black males were really thrust into male/female situations as opposed to

JOHN MCCLUSKEY, JR.

having some concrete ideas of how to go about getting married. At an early age—eighteen and nineteen, let's say—the thing that attracts a black male to a woman is not really love. It's more how the woman looks, or he has some sexual overtones in mind, and usually what happens is the two get together and do it. There really isn't love involved in seeking out a mate. I think what I'm saying is that black men don't seek out a mate in terms of choosing a good, reliable woman. They just fall into a situation. I think that's partly why relationships among blacks don't really last. In fact, I think previously we were hit with the idea of women having babies out of wedlock at a very young age, and the whole idea has become catastrophic among blacks because there are so many black teenage girls walking around with their stomach sticking out and no husband or no man in sight. I always wonder, where is the father? That goes back to the whole idea of the family structure, and that's one thing that I think has been decaying among blacks. The family structure was really the basis of black survival. Now you have girls getting pregnant at thirteen. I know of a case.

J. Mc.: You would think that this would be passed down by sisters and even brothers, that the women would be getting more streetwise.

WALTER: But streetwise really starts at home. Where were the girl's values and all that were supposed to be taught at home, and conversely, where were the man's? When I was coming up, sex was not an openly discussed thing, it was really rather taboo. Girls were real afraid of it, and the male, too. We used to talk a lot about this and that and be lying and all about, "Man, I had this one, I had that one." But it was all just talk. But we're really living in troubled times now where everything is open. And I think that that has really hurt me—the black woman in a larger sense, the whole idea of freedom and independence. I often hear women, particularly since the advent of the women's lib movement, say that the black woman was liberated a long time ago. But I'm not really so sure of that.

J. Mc.: Yeah, you hear that all the time.

WALTER: It's really a catastrophe what's happening to the black male/female relationship. But who do you blame? Do you blame the woman, or do you blame the man? I don't really know the answer to that, but I don't really think that's the question to ask, because the damage has been done. And one of the hardest things to do is to go backwards. But a lot of times that's what needs to be done—we need to go back to the old ways. Going back seems to be a hard thing to do for anything in life. I think we're really at a crossroads in terms of male/female relationships.

J. Mc.: What about in your own personal sense of self?

WALTER: To give you a little background, my father died at an early age. So from the age of nineteen, it was just my mother, and I have an older sister and two younger brothers. I was relatively pretty big and I was away at school, so I consider this as being out of the house by eighteen. Except for the holidays and my father's funeral, for a complete four years I was away and just coming home for holidays. Then after school I came home; I stayed only a year, and then I moved to New York. This was all in Florida.

In terms of the male/female relationship thing, I met my wife while in college. In fact, I guess it could be characterized as being my college sweetheart. I met her on campus, and we started dating. At that age I think there was no . . . but a lot of dating and going out together. When I graduated, I left her there because she was a year behind me. She would come to visit me in Jacksonville because her home town was just outside of Jacksonville. We were happy with that, and I think this held true during those times we were talking about in the sixties. The

JOHN MCCLUSKEY, JR.

point was that if you were really dating a girl or seeing her for any extended length of time, you were expected to marry her. There was no question of do you love her or anything, is this the person that you seek out. I really didn't give much thought to marrying her. It's just that the ideas and attitudes and the civilization of the time seemed to dictate that that's what you were supposed to do, so that's what I did. There was nothing about love or anything. It was just following what was socially acceptable—and especially in light of the fact that we had been sleeping together. She finished school, we got married, and then we decided to come to New York to seek our fortune. I've never been in love before, and I've been married now twenty-nine years.

J. Mc.: Is that right? That's good.

WALTER: You say that's good, but what you're really saying is that you're happy that it lasted that long. I'm not really sure about the good part. She and I have broken up, but people of modern-day generations would be divorced six or seven times by now. But to really hold a relationship together, you have to have those old school values; I think you try harder.

When I met her she had a son, and he was just a couple years old. Once we got married we had another son together, and that has been the only kids. I'm thankful that we were able to raise those two.

J. Mc.: So they're grown now?

WALTER: Yes. One is a career serviceman, and the other one is here in New York; he just finished college, and he's working now for the transit. Our first relationship, between her and me, I think is a pretty good one. But we really don't have mutual interests or things that we do together. The type of people that I like to hang with are usually different from the types that she likes to hang around. So we've grown apart. I guess one good thing about getting married at such an early age is that we would have grown together, but not so. I've always been kind of the uppity persuasion, as she might call it. For example, I like the arts, opera. I like the high-class upper style of living. My friends generally tend to be financially secure. I hang with a lot of Wall Street executives and go to parties where there are society people, and I feel quite comfortable in those settings, because that's how I view myself as wanting to be. I'm a registered Republican, and I have been all my life. I tend to gravitate to the upper-echelon people and have no discriminatory values in terms of black or white. I have a lot of white friends and hang out with a white group as quick as I will a black, and we relate and get along together. I like riding in limousines or taking a trip to some exotic place, where she really likes the common people and, as a person, gravitates that way. So that's the point that I was trying to make in terms of drifting apart in ideas and attitudes: she would try to save money and buy the cheapest cuts of meat, where I would not give a second thought to going out to eat at a fancy expensive restaurant.

J. Mc.: So the question is how to find a happy medium in that circumstance.

WALTER: No, not really, because I don't think I'm seeking to reach a happy medium. It's been so many years now that I don't think I'm looking for a medium anymore. I'm just doing my thing and she's doing her thing. I will go to Hawaii on vacation, where to her that may seem extravagant. I am at a loss to understand why she feels that way. I could understand if we didn't have the finances, but if you can afford those things, then my view is why not?

ROBERT

ROBERT: Maybe it's the grandmothers who shape the Afro-American male. I can't say recently, but like the sixties or seventies. Then when it got to be the eighties and now into the nineties, grandmothers are going out. I'm speaking of those without fathers, cause you have a situation where the male leaves, and there you have grandmothers and mothers. The grandmother's the backbone, and the mother is in there pushing this male forward. I'd say dentists, lawyers, athletes, they really were pushed by their mothers, and I know of one story here that just hit the paper in New York. There was an argument in Brooklyn, and this guy whipped out a gun and shot a little nine-year-old girl—shot her right through the car and into her head. We found out she died today. He was a promising ballplayer in the minor leagues with a career right there before him, and this was a situation where he lost his cool.

J. Mc.: Was this a family situation?

ROBERT: No, it wasn't family—it was an accident in the street; whether it was a fender-bender I don't know. He just got angry and lost his cool. He went back to his car and pulled out a gun, and naturally an angry man with a gun doesn't really hit his target. Bullets flew all over the place. One shot right through the car and hit this girl that was asleep on the seat. Some of the young men today that are coming up just lose their tempers too much. Here was this girl and she's hit and dead, and he had a promising career but now he's down the tubes.

J. Mc.: That's a tragic story. In situations like that, you were saying that it was the grandmother, born in the South in the rural areas, not in the cities, who kept people in check.

ROBERT: That's right. And some of this rubbed off on the mothers, see? But as you got into the eighties you didn't see it no more. I see a lot of mothers, instead of discipline they're giving their children everything that they ask for. Then when the child grows up, he doesn't have this discipline; he doesn't have this going to school to earn and all that, and next thing you know he's probably out here in the street dealing drugs. And he's buying his own of what he wants. It could be a Jeep, it could be a motorcycle, because the money is coming in fast, so naturally what goes with it is the clothes, too. And they're not having another thing that grandmothers instilled in us too, and that is

61

the faith in God. Even some of the mothers would take you to church, and faith in God was instilled there. But in the eighties, you didn't see that too much. That's something that's really gone. And they're just giving, giving, and then they wonder why tragedies happen in their family. I read somewhere that the more you put God out, the more your adversary takes control. He's looking to get you any way he can.

J. Mc.: Where do you think that break came? You were saying that it was one way twenty years ago and a different way in the eighties and nineties.

ROBERT: Yeah, eighties into the nineties. There are very few now who are raised in the fear of God, and very few have that grandmother thing that we had in the fifties and sixties.

J. Mc.: Maybe it was that individual who was aware of the old ways when families were closer physically because of living in small quarters or in the rural South. I'm just trying to get a fix on their commitment in the church and how that stayed together after the move up north.

ROBERT: But you just gave me something too. There can be closeness in the family. If there were three to five kids, or even eight to thirteen kids, there was also a closeness in the family because love knitted us together. I know of some cases where there's four kids and five kids in the family, and one goes this way and one goes that way, and "I'm going out and that's it." But I know of another case where this woman always took her children to church, and they are grown now, in their early and late twenties. They are good kids; they don't even dress like the children of today dress with these Nikes and all of that. They wear suits and ties, and the daughter wears nice dresses. That was a close-knit family. I remember on Mother's Day, they wrote a beautiful letter to their father and mother, about how you didn't have no education and you sacrificed things for us. But the main thing that I noticed in that letter was the love that the mother and father had and how he held this family together.

JOHN MCCLUSKEY, JR.

Whereas today, I've seen the same situation but the children are younger. I can see them coming up and they're saying, "No, I'm going outside"; there isn't that closeness in the family—they fuss and fight.

J. Mc.: Is there anything that you want to add?

ROBERT: I know you said something about girlfriends, and I know that some guys have the girlfriends too. A man can have a wife and children, too, and he might meet another woman. Through this other woman he can see where he is wrong and go back home, or maybe he just gets tired of her and goes back home.

J. Mc.: Which made him get a new light on what he was doing.

ROBERT: Yes. Like one time he's on the inside looking out, and then when he gets on the outside he begins looking in, you know? Like I try to tell these guys, especially these young married men, you go with these women here and they only want you until the eleven o'clock news comes on; after that you can go on home, because it's the sexual need and companionship that the lonely woman wants. After the news comes on, it's "You get on out of here"; two more nights will go by, or three or four nights, and then you can come up and see her again. That's the situation that I see. I try to tell these guys, don't get involved in it, because you're wasting your substance and part of your life with this other woman. It could be for two years, it could be for three or four years, but when it finally hits you—bam! When you go back, it's not the same as it was when you first got together.

J. Mc.: I'm curious about the person now in a new role. Are fathers saying anything different to their daughters? The point you just made opened up that whole question.

ROBERT: I sat down with my daughter and her friend, and we talked about the question of living together. I said, hey, some time ago I did this thing too, and I'll tell you right now it's not

63

going to work out. You're either going to get married or you're not. It's God blesses the marriage, but staying together without the marriage, that's not something that is blessed. In God's sight it could be sanctioned that man and woman get together, but on earth you have to have the paper that says "I do mean to" and all of that. When you just live together, it's like I can take a walk, I can go any time I wish. I spoke to them about religion and sex and I laid it down. You know this man, but do you really *know* this man?

FRED

J. Mc.: Would you discuss the role of the female in the shaping and development of the African American male? That can be both a general question and a personal one.

FRED: It's my personal feeling that the black woman really doesn't know how to raise a black male child. She does a great job with a daughter, but she falls very short in dealing with the black male—and I say that for many reasons. She teaches him how to be honest, but honesty is not always the best policy because she doesn't know anything about politics. I'm speaking on the whole. I think music is black people's worst enemy. Eighty percent of the young girls that listen to this have got babies out of wedlock, they've got little girlfriends, right? And before the kid can learn his ABC's and learn fundamental education, the first thing he sees is someone shaking they behinds. When I was a teenager, a cracker told me one time, "You know why your people dance so good, Fred?" I said, "Yeah, cause we've got rhythm." He said, "No, because all your brains are in your ass." And the older I get, the more I believe it.

J. Mc.: Was this in Georgia or was this in New York?

FRED: This cracker told me this in San Antonio, Texas, in 1955, and I have never forgot it. He was a funny cracker, and he was a small cracker too. And I beat the cracker up, and that's one

JOHN MCCLUSKEY, JR.

thing that I'm ashamed of today, because that cracker sure told me the truth. You know what he told me one time? He said, "You know the difference between a cracker woman going to a beauty parlor and a nigger woman going? The nigger woman going to get the crimps out and the cracker woman going to get them in." You know the idea—the man was insane. He was insane and insulting, but the damnedest thing in the world happened when I left there to go to Montana—guess who they sent with me? And we went in a restaurant and they didn't want to serve me, and he wouldn't eat. It'll show you what a short time can do with people.

In terms of my personal development, I think we discussed that before. I told you people in the neighborhood convinced my mother that she was raising a nut, that there was something wrong with me. And my mama went for it. John, this is very personal. Let me show you how things can happen. You know how I ended up in the hospital? I was a straight A student, and I had a principal who was brutal. I hated the son of a bitch. I wished to God that I could've been a man, because I would have killed him twice. He took a personal dislike to me, and he attacked me and brutalized me in front of the whole student body. I ran away from home and went to Florida on my own. I was gone for three or four months.

J. Mc.: Because of the principal?

FRED: Yeah. And when I got back, my mama sent me to the reformatory for truancy. She called herself helping me by sending me there with a bunch of criminals. Let me tell you, I've always had a lot of heart, and this pulled a lot of meanness out of me. And to show you just how things were, you know I missed a year and a half of school. When I came back—I think this is the proudest thing that ever happened to me in my life—I was going to that reformatory for a whole school year, and my class had gone on before me, and I scored the highest marks of anybody in the school. I got a 96 for the whole semester. You can check that out; it's recorded. That was the tenth grade/sophomore year. I only got about 90 something after that; I never scored that high again. But it was a matter of I had to do something to prove to myself.

J. Mc.: And then you came to New York after that?

FRED: No, I went into the military.

J. Mc.: What about after the military? What about relationships with women after and during the military?

FRED: Well, John, I know a lot about a lot of women, but I wouldn't want to talk about it. Cause remember one thing, a gentleman should always respect a lady. Whatever happens with a man and woman is always private and personal. I am going to tell you something, I've got a little legacy. I've got a grandmother that I'm really proud of. I had a grandfather who was big in the Church of Christ. He set up a college in Tennessee, and the president was my grandfather's best friend, but it was my grandmother pushing my grandfather. Her name was Francis Mattren. She had a girlfriend that lived in Hay City, Florida, and she had a girlfriend who lived in Daytona Beach, Florida, named Mary McLeod Bethune. In 1944 I had the opportunity of eating in her house.

J. Mc.: *The* Mary McLeod Bethune?

FRED: That's right, I sat on her knee, boy. I've had some great things happen to me in my life. Do you remember Big Joe Turner out of St. Louis, Missouri? He never seen me but three or four times in his life, but he was serious fun to me. They had this joint called the Blue Note in Valdosta, and all of the top entertainers used to come there. And the dude that owned the joint, he'd let me come the day after the parties when I got out of school. He'd let me clean up the place and take the money to the bank. The money he was giving me was a lot of money at that time. I got into conversations with Joe Turner and he was impressed, and every time he would come there he would always

JOHN MCCLUSKEY, JR.

wait for me. We would go to this place called Tommy Mazies, and we'd sit down and talk. He'd tell me, "I don't know what you're going to be when you grow up, but you ought to be something." Let me tell you, I've failed Joe and myself.

PATRICK

PATRICK: The women in my life when I was growing up played a major role. As I said before, we're not originally from this country. We're from Costa Rica, so it's more like coming from a different lifestyle, where you were much poorer than here. We didn't have so many things as they have here, so my mother got it from her grandmother, making use of what little she has—if it means baking or if it means going in the back yard and picking fruit from the trees that we had and trying to sell it in the market. I learned a lot of good qualities from my mother even though we didn't have a good relationship. Sometimes I feel like my mother was young when she had us—I mean like not prepared. She wasn't ready to deal with children. I can tell this by the impatient attitude that she had towards us; even at a young age I noticed this. My father was the one that we could always turn to and get answers to our questions. It's really the mother who should play that role, but in our family it was different. I got a lot of strong qualities from my mother: There's no such word as "you can't"; even if you earn twenty dollars a week, you can always put a dollar aside. And these are things that stay with me today. My father is so proud—if he can't have it this way, he'd rather not have it at all. But my mother taught me how to be strong, how to do for myself. When my father used to try to spoil us, my mother would chop us down. It was good. I couldn't see it then, but I really appreciate it now.

J. Mc.: Did anything change when your family moved from Costa Rica to New York?

PATRICK: There was no change as far as my mother's concerned; she's always been the same. If she didn't like something, she would tell you about it. My sisters, we had such a strict upbringing that it was pathetic. All of the other kids could do what they wanted, and we couldn't because we had something embedded in our minds. We grew up with our grandmother in Costa Rica before we came to the U.S., and our father and mother came here first. Therefore, I didn't spend the first five or six years with my mother or father. I spent them with my grandmother, so that's who really molded me. She was so strict in the way that she did things, and she just didn't play games. So we had the proper upbringing, but not from our parents. When we came here to the United States, we were considered goody two-shoes. Everybody else was doing what they wanted, but we just couldn't do it. Come six o'clock we had to come inside. It's time for the news, so it's time to come inside. Before you eat, time to wash up. Eight-thirty or nine P.M., time to go to bed, and before you go to bed you say your prayers. It was kind of like an army, but then we had fun, too. My sisters are the ones that I feel closest to today because my parents, my mother, had such a regimented style of bringing up children. I didn't feel I could go to her for a lot of things. The things that I value now were what I was taught then, but I've never had that open relationship with my mother. So I had it with my sisters. And I've grown to respect my sisters in a way that I don't hear many people talk about.

J. Mc.: Do they both live in New York?

PATRICK: One lives upstate in Kingston, New York, and one lives in Virginia. Very, very ambitious; we get that from my father. Very ambitious and business-minded. And from my mother we incorporated both sides. One of my sisters, she'll take anything and make a dollar. She went down to Virginia and picked up some pine and went to the store and picked up baskets and towels and stuff, and now she started making pottery—I mean crafts, country products, and she's got a mail-order busi-

JOHN MCCLUSKEY, JR.

ness that way. She's making money. The natural talent of the family is art. We can all draw, we can all do sculpture. She draws, and she does graphics for her company. She puts together little tiny ads for candy bars and stuff like that. That's how she makes a little commission. She don't get it all of the time, but when she does, it comes in good. That comes from my mother, but the business part comes from my father. That's the way that I am, too. I have an older sister, and she's the same way. But she's more family-oriented, and that's where my mother comes in—a lot more family-oriented and a lot less on the business side, and the way she got far in life is based on the strict upbringing. I respect my sisters for that. I could go to them and talk to them about anything. If it wasn't for them, I would keep it all to myself, because I just don't feel people understand me.

J. Mc.: It's good to have that relationship. A lot of people can't say that about members of their own family. Anything with other females that you know? I think that you already implied in terms of communication that it's with your sisters.

PATRICK: Right. As far as my grandmother's concerned, she was the standard by which all things were set. Like I said, my mother had us when she was young; she didn't know what to do. My grandmother was the one who stepped in and did a lot of things. Qualities that we have originate from my grandmother and the values and things that she taught us to do for ourselves. Keep a tight relationship with Christ and God. Even though I wandered off doing some crazy things, my own things, I knew in the back of my mind the way I was taught, so I always came back to it.

As far as dealing with women on the outside, I really can't say too much. I always try to measure women that I go out with against my sisters. If they don't fit the standards that my sisters fit, I don't pursue too much. It seems like I have had a lot of relationships, but they were more like one-night stands. It was more of a sexual thing than a commitment or understanding kind of thing. I've never run into a woman that had the qualities that I was looking for, so until then I'm just shopping around.

I did work for quite a few females. When I was in the army with the field medics, I had a sergeant I will never forget because she was everything all rolled into one. She was a sergeant, she was a sister. And she had a different method of getting people to respect her—her method of getting people to react to her was just bending an ear. And just not treating people like the army treats them—like one person would use the same method for everybody. She looked at people as individuals, and to get them to do what she wanted them to do, she would adjust herself to that person. And it didn't matter what it took to get to that point. She wouldn't bend backwards for anybody. She wasn't a softy. I admired her because I couldn't see how she could be a woman and retain her femininity and still get the most out of it. People listened to her and respected her. She stood up to people. She stood up to sergeants, she stood up to colonels, she stood up to a lot of different people that other people would not stand up to.

After that I worked at St. John's Hospital. My boss was around thirty-eight to forty years old, and at the time I was maybe twenty-two. And you know, when I worked with her, I learned quite a few things from her. She's a real funny lady. She's a real teaser, so to speak, because she's forty and looks twenty and she knows it. She too knew how to get people to do certain things, and she was a motivator within the whole group. I picked up a lot from her also, I really did.

* * *

After the last set of interviews and during the transcription period, I attempted to keep in contact with all five men. Within two years of the interviews, Paul died. Without the assistance of Paul Thomas, Jr., this interview with this group of men could not have taken place. Patrick left New York within a year of the interview and was living in Vir-

JOHN MCCLUSKEY, JR.

ginia at last report. I have lost contact with Robert. I am still in touch with Walter and Fred.

During the initial interview, I was struck by how easily the men shared their experiences and located common ground. Key refrains were the deadliness of the term "nigger" and any putdown designation; the urgency of economic autonomy; the necessity of firm and loving parenting—with special and consistent mention of the maternal grandmother; and a blues-like optimism about their own lives and those close to them.

I would like to thank the Ford Foundation and the Afro-American Studies Department at Indiana University–Bloomington for support during the preparation of the interview transcript.

Munich Olympic Games

3. Five Friends

Let us address the crisis among African American men by looking at five childhood friends. These five men were born in a poor neighborhood in the inner city. All of the families on their street were headed by single mothers, some divorced, and others never married, with most receiving some sort of welfare. In many cases the children never even knew their fathers. These five boys played together, spent time at each other's houses, and attended the same schools. But although they have much in common, they have turned out very differently, depending in part on how they have utilized the tools and resources in their environment, and how they have reacted to and compensated for some of the missing basic elements.

Morris is the son of a woman named Bernadine. She herself grew up in a home without a father, and in her constant search for the male attention she had missed out on, she found herself being used and abused a lot by men. At the age of eighteen she fell madly in love with Morris's father, but when he found out she was pregnant, he did the paper doll—he cut out. Bernadine was mad and confused and felt terribly hurt and betrayed. She then learned that he had been sleeping with her best friend on the side. All of this, added to her earlier bad experiences with men and her already low level of self-worth, made her decide that men "weren't shit."

Her negative experiences with men unfortunately carried over into her relationship with her son. So Morris grew up hearing a constant negative, destructive refrain that became embedded in his mind: "Your daddy was a no good son of a bitch." "I hope you're not going to be like that motherfucker." "Black men ain't shit." "Your daddy was no good, and you're going to be just like him."

As a child, Morris went occasionally to church, but his attendance dropped as he got older and lost interest. His performance in school wasn't great, and with nothing to inspire or motivate him to do better, he eventually dropped out to do what he saw his peers doing—nothing. He had very little in his life to make him feel like he was somebody. In addition to his mother's harsh judgments of black men, there was nothing from his culture that touched him on a daily or weekly basis, that said, "You're important; you're special." Instead the opposite was reinforced.

Morris did not grow up in a family situation where he had close contact with his grandparents—seeing them grow old, retire, and enjoy their golden years fishing, traveling, and doing constructive things. The men he saw around him did nothing to make him look forward to advancing past the age of twenty-five; most of the men thirty-five and older were so beaten up from many years of abusing drugs and being in jail that they looked like they were in their seventies. Penniless and on the streets, they were still going from door to door, house to house, shuckin' and jivin'.

So there was nothing in Morris's environment that made him feel important as a black person, as a man, or as a religious person. He grew up with a yearning inside, a feeling of being unfulfilled that he didn't understand. There was a desire to be "stroked," to be told and made to feel that he was important, that he was loved, that he was special. He eventually joined a gang, just to feel that he belonged somewhere, and as part of his initiation he robbed someone. What happened? The gang members told him that he was cool. "That's great!" they said. "You are a

WILBERT JORDAN

tough man!" That made him feel good, so in order to get more encouragement, he robbed someone else and began committing increasingly more serious crimes. At last he had found his essence. At last he was someone.

Morris is not very loving, and we shouldn't expect him to be. He has not experienced much love in his life. He saw and heard a number of men come in and out to be with his mother, but that wasn't love. He himself is not very sexual; sex for him is more of a control thing. His sexual encounters are usually brief, rough, and insensitive. He often beats or slaps his women, under the guise that they cannot understand him, or they tried to resist him. "No" is not in his vocabulary unless you have the power to back it up. So "his women" don't say "No" or "Stop." They are his bitches and whores, and that's how he treats them.

Morris has no sense of right and wrong as we know it. He grew up with little guidance; most of what he heard in his childhood were negatives, don'ts. Rarely was there an encouraging word. For him, happiness has been experienced only when he has taken from others. In his mind, he has already conceded that he will be dead by age thirty. So he has very little to look forward to. The fact that he can have nice jewelry, clothing, and cars for a few years is a dream come true. From the outside we keep singing "Just say no" and "Get a job," phrases with no meaning to Morris. Why would he say no? At last he has some pride in himself—not because he is black, not because he is American, but because he is a member of his gang. That is his identity. That is what is important.

Morris's childhood friend Darryl grew up just a few houses down the street. From the time Darryl was a baby, people were always raving about how cute he was. Everywhere he went, his looks attracted attention. Darryl's primary male role model when he was growing up was his mother's brother Todd, who was gay. He took many of his mannerisms from Todd and at an early age began to express some effeminate gestures.

One evening Darryl went across the street to play with his

cousin Carl. Carl's father answered the door, invited Darryl inside, then told him that Carl and his mother were out shopping. As Darryl turned to go, his uncle put his hand on the door and smiled, telling him, "No. Today I'm going to teach you something." He took Darryl downstairs and molested him, telling him that this was what he deserved because he was so cute.

Initially Darryl tried to fight back against his uncle. But molestation is not a sexual act; it is an assertion of power and control, and Darryl's resistance afforded his uncle the chance to be even more dominating and to further humiliate his young nephew. Darryl was forced to comply orally with his uncle, then was embarrassed when the older man compared the size of their genitals. His manhood was further diminished when his uncle wrestled him down, looked him in the eye, and told him what he was going to do to him, and that he had better like it because he was going to get it every week from then on.

For the next seven years, Darryl was molested by his uncle. He never told anyone, feeling that he was the guilty one, and thinking that he deserved what was happening to him. In time, his spirit bruised and battered, he voluntarily went over. He didn't feel like a man; he had no sense of himself other than as a passive sexual partner. He grew increasingly effeminate and became sharp-tongued and self-destructive, struggling to find an identity—but the only identity he could find was as "a good lay."

As the years passed, Darryl became more open and developed into a very effeminate gay man, actively seeking out sexual partners. Ironically, most of the men he gets involved with are married, like the uncle who molested him. He goes from one partner to another in a desperate but futile search for the self-esteem he has never felt—and will never find in his steady stream of almost faceless sexual encounters.

Darryl frankly doesn't know how to love. He has been severely scarred mentally. Every time he submits passively to sex with another partner, his lowly position is reinforced; he is

WILBERT JORDAN

always the one servicing or being used, never the recipient of a loving touch. His life is filled with stories of giving men money, being hurt and abused, and he has drowned this out as the years have gone by with drugs and booze.

As a black homosexual, Darryl has a compounded negative self-image. "Gay" is a term adopted by the white homosexual community and is not widely used within the black community. More commonly used are terms like "funny," "affected," "sissy," "one of the children." None of these words bother Darryl on the surface; he has been called all of them. But inside they add subtly to his damaged sense of self.

Nor does Darryl have anything in his life to make him feel proud as a black man—or even as a man at all. He sees few blacks in any position of power; money and success are something that the whites have. If you're black and are lucky enough to be successful, it's because you've kissed some white man's ass. So in his mind, being white is better than being black. What is good about being black? Frankly, Darryl can't tell you.

Booker grew up in the house next door to Morris. A sensitive boy and an only child, he was hungry for his mother's love, but she was always too preoccupied with the men in her life to pay attention to him. A second-generation welfare mother, she had never worked; instead she spent her days entertaining a succession of men. Young Booker would watch as they got his mother drunk and seduced her. One day he walked into the house to find his mother and some new man in the throes of drunken passion. The man looked back over his shoulder at Booker and smiled as he continued thrusting into his mother. And as he was leaving, he stopped and said to Booker: "I know she is yo mama, but to me she is just a piece of ass." That image and those words were forever imprinted in the boy's mind.

So Booker began to look elsewhere for the female affection he craved. He was badly hurt by the first girl he truly fell in love with when he found out that she was using him for the nice things he would buy and do for her, and that she actually was in love with and sleeping with somebody else. Booker's trust was shaken, and from that time on he approached women as conquests and nothing more. He had noticed how easily taken in his mother and her friends were by the attentions of a charming man, and he soon learned that this approach would work well for him, too. Flattery and smooth talk really could get a man almost anywhere, it seemed. He became sexually promiscuous, moving from one woman to the next, taking what he wanted (and enjoying the hollow high of momentarily winning the female attention that he so badly needed) and giving little in return—except for the eight kids he now has by five different women.

Like Darryl, Booker is caught up in a vicious cycle—searching for self-esteem and a sense of himself as a man in a way that can never lead to it. He is not a good writer. He is not creative, except when it comes to luring a new woman into bed. He is not an exceptional dancer. He will never develop a new method of accounting or teaching math to inner-city children. With his welfare-dependent mother as his only role model when he was growing up, he never had reason to develop a work ethic of any kind. His essence lies between his legs and in his ability to manipulate women.

The fourth of our five friends is Leonard. Like the others, he grew up with a single mother. Although she loved him and tried to be there for him, she was usually too busy with her part-time job at a fast-food restaurant and with her other children to spend the individual time with her son that he needed. But Leonard was lucky, because he got to spend a lot of time with his paternal grandmother and great-grandmother, who lived close by and doted on him. Consequently, many of the people he had a lot of contact with were older and more mature, with a sense of value and direction.

He heard stories about his grandfather—what kind of work he did, what kind of man he was. He saw his grandmother at an older age in a healthy environment, still active and still making plans for her life. Twice an elderly couple invited him to accompany them on a cross-country trip, which helped him to expand his horizons beyond his immediate environment—he learned that there was a greater world. Implanted in Leonard's mind was the idea that life is a continuum, and he could have fun when he was forty, fifty, sixty, even seventy. There was a lot to look forward to in the future.

His older friends also piqued his interest in black history. Hearing them speak with pride about Jackie Robinson, Mary McLeod Bethune, and many others made him want to learn more about his ancestors. That quest led him to the library, where he eagerly pursued his interest. And as he learned about the richness of black history, he began to learn about himself. This strengthened his identity as an individual and as a black man.

Quiet and fairly studious, he also was the recipient of a fair amount of positive attention for his efforts at school. Even when his mother was too busy to understand and pay attention, Grandma and Great-Grandma were there to encourage him and say good things, to help him feel good about himself. So he continued to strive. He wasn't an A student bound for Harvard or MIT, but with the help and encouragement of the people in his life, he graduated from high school and went on to the city college.

Leonard is more loving than the others, mainly because he grew up with more examples of concern and compassion and love. He was held by his grandmother and great-grandmother. He was hugged, kissed, and greeted with a smile. He received love as we know it and is able to reciprocate love—he is the only one of the five friends to have married. He is somebody. He believes that, and he knows about himself and who he is. He knows he is loved and how to love. He is able to communicate and contribute to the greater black society. He is a *man*.

The fifth friend, J.C., is a professional athlete now. He grew up having to cope with the noise of four siblings at home, and to escape the chaos he often played ball in the streets or over at the playground until the sun went down. And he played hard—it was his unconscious way of getting so tired that when he went home he could sleep with no distraction. It's not easy to sleep on a couch in the living room when your brother is watching TV, a cousin is on the phone, the radio is playing, people are talking and laughing, and someone has the stereo going—you've got to be tired to go to sleep!

J.C. has made it in the world of athletics. But he has very little sense of himself as a black man. He has never heard anything great about his blackness, only about his athletic skills. He can remember being addressed with "Nigger, what's up?" And when his mother got mad, she would say, "Boy, get your black ass up; you're late for school." But he doesn't really understand what being black means. He is not aware of W. E. B. Du Bois, Frederick Douglass, or Booker T. Washington. He knows nothing of Africa or its glorious past. He doesn't know that there are blacks in Brazil. He has little sense of the history of slavery. He *does* know how to play basketball, how to run, how to hit a baseball—but he knows nothing of the problems of Joe Louis or the accomplishments of Jackie Robinson or Althea Gibson.

J.C.'s skills have brought him success, and along the way he has come to identify as a man. Are we surprised, then, to find that he chose a non-black for his wife? Why would he marry a black woman? That's like saying he can't be a total man and go where he wants to go. It's the Rolls Royce syndrome at work.

In black culture, the male-female relationship is competitive. Black music, particularly the blues, reflects this view. The black man often conquers his female partner and then, when sharing his exploits with friends, exaggerates how well he has pleased her. In Western culture the black man is often reputed to have near-legendary sexual prowess, but he has never been viewed as a gentle, passionate lover. The black female thus can pull the rug out from under him. One negative remark about his sexual abilities, and all of his exploits can be destroyed.

The white female is different. The very fact that the black

WILBERT JORDAN

man has a white woman says to his peers that he is good; why else would "the woman" be with him? If a rich man drives into Beverly Hills in a Pontiac and wants the people he sees to know his status, he will have to do a lot of talking to convince them. But if he drives there in a Rolls Royce, his car will say it all. For many black men, a white woman serves the same function.

It is obvious that I have greatly generalized these five men. I have done so to dramatize the power of early influences and structure in their lives. However, my work at the Charles Drew–Martin Luther King, Jr. Medical Center and with HIV-positive populations in Los Angeles validates the *range* of these types. This is based on my knowledge of and interviews with more than three thousand patients. Of the patients seen in the OASIS Clinic, 88 percent are male and 12 percent female, and about 20 percent are transgender. Of the men, 44 percent reveal a strong history of molestation; in fact, when the effeminate men in the clinic—those who exhibit exaggerated feminine gestures and refer to themselves using terms such as "girl"—have been asked if they were raped by a friend or family member, all of them (100 percent) have answered in the affirmative.

Interestingly, interviews with the sisters of these men reveal that a significant number were themselves molested by the same person who molested their brother. Even more dramatic is the fact that often each sibling was allowing the abuse to happen to him- or herself in order to protect the other, not realizing that the sibling was also being molested. This most commonly occurs in single-parent homes, most often by mothers' boyfriends, stepbrothers, older cousins, and uncles. Older brothers are also frequently implicated; only rarely is the father involved.

It is not necessary to grow up in a two-parent home to be stable and productive. Children can certainly be raised successfully by a single parent (and unsuccessfully by two parents). Many a child who was raised by a struggling young single mother has gone on to be successful and contribute positively to society. But there are factors that must interplay with that child

81

while he or she is young that will guarantee such a meaningful end. When children are raised with very little structure and very little input about what it means to have an identity, it is unreasonable to expect very much of them.

Leonard was raised around elderly people who told him about black people and about black history. This gave him a sense of what being black was, and pride in his heritage. Though the information he was given was not as structured as that received by Jewish and Chinese children, who attend weekend schools where they are taught their history in detail, it was enough to make him feel that being black was important. All too often, however, black children do not grow up among people who can impart to them the positive values of being black. If they get any positive input at all, the emphasis may be, as it was for J.C., on their athletic abilities or other talents, or they may be given a strong religious foundation while the importance of their ethnic heritage is ignored. This can cause them to have a sense of self-esteem that is based only in their athletic skills or their religion rather than their ethnicity. The danger is that they may still feel negative about being black and will then seek non-black mates.

If at some later point in Darryl's life he was lucky enough to encounter experiences that made him feel good about being gay, he would still not feel good about being black, because the foundation for that sense of self-pride was not laid when he was young. Likewise, even if Morris could find a way to rise above his life of crime, he probably would still lack any sense of pride in himself as a black man. They would then do what most people in this situation do—migrate to an all-white environment.

Black culture developed in the context of a segregated system in the South. In its classic form, it is rural. Because it was a culture of slaves and of a disenfranchised people, it was not perfect, nor did it have its chance to be so. But it had structures in place to enable its members to develop self-pride. When there were emotional problems, for example, help was sought

WILBERT JORDAN

from a spiritualist or voodoo priest. As blacks began to migrate from the rural to an urban environment and moved from a legally segregated system into an "integrated" one, the role of the spiritualist or priest diminished. As a result, for many African Americans there is no longer anyone considered adequate to deal with emotional problems, since black culture has historically viewed psychiatrists and psychologists as doctors who deal with "crazy people." We now have a void left by the declining use of priests and spiritualists, yet no structured movement exists to incorporate psychiatry and psychology.

The segregated schools went beyond teaching the three R's; they also taught pride and were the source for blacks to learn about African and African American history. Although the history that was taught may have varied from one school to the next, it imparted many positive values. Schoolteachers served as surrogate parents, often encouraging pupils to go on to college or to take up a trade; sometimes they even took the initiative to obtain the necessary scholarships. As we urbanized and integrated, this valuable resource, too, was lost.

The greatness of the late Dr. Benjamin Mays of Morehouse College consisted not in his skill at writing scholarly articles, but in that he was the quintessential father figure. He, more than any other black college president, singly inspired and molded many young black men. He was able to individualize the needs of his students and provide for each that unfinished fathering. When a culture lacks a structure to teach its history and thereby give its people a feeling of pride and dignity, it is very difficult to expect anyone to have a positive self-image. There is no argument that integration and the passage of the Civil Rights Bill led to many opportunities for black Americans. But we must face the fact that though we gained much, we also suffered some important losses.

Many blacks view themselves positively with respect to their religion. Members of the Nation of Islam have a dual positive image: they see themselves as great because they are black, and great because they are Muslim. Many black Christians, in contrast, have a sense of self-worth about being Christian, but not about being black.

The spectrum of religion in the black community is broad and enthusiastic, sometimes approaching fanatical. I believe that the reason for this lies partly in the lack of self-esteem, but also in history. Too often those who have been saved, whatever denomination they may be, feel that they possess nearly a manifest destiny. The members of the smallest storefront church may well strongly believe that they are the only people that God is going to take to heaven, and the rest of the world is wrong. That is a common phenomenon among both black and white Pentecostals and Fundamentalists, and even the Nationalists have that sort of black churchism, with each group believing that they are "right" and the others "wrong." This is because these people's self-knowledge is lacking and out of balance; all their essence is in this one thing. People who have no self-esteem and are suddenly made to feel important after converting to a religion or movement can become fanatical—their whole identity is that conversion, that membership; it is the only thing that gives them a feeling of importance and righteousness.

It is imperative that we begin to impart a sense of cultural context, of African American history, so that we all can learn to appreciate other movements as well as our own. Such self-destructive fanaticism is often viewed as being self-hatred, and in a way it is—but the reason is that these people have never been taught to like others; they can like only those who are part of the same movement. They lack self-knowledge, a sense of history, and an understanding and appreciation of their broader culture. We need to have church schools teach black history and black pride. I believe that a summit is paramount. This would allow us to do two important things: (1) define our desired cultural outcomes, such as self-confidence, aggressiveness, and group cohesiveness, and (2) list ways in which these outcomes can be achieved, such as teaching African and African Ameri-

WILBERT JORDAN

can history to our youth, teaching our teenagers and young adults how to be spouses and parents, teaching black music and art appreciation.

One of the great benefits the Muslims brought to a disenfranchised and economically and educationally unsophisticated group of urban people was teaching their members how to be parents, how to be husband and wife. Until our culture contains elements that guarantee that people being raised in it will have at least some exposure to certain values that will make them loving, help them to become good parents, make them caring, show them how to be encouraging of children rather than destructive and discouraging, we will not see kids progress. Too many black children hear statements like "You ain't shit; you ain't nothing; you ain't going to be nothing." If a teacher asks a class of black children what they want to be, and someone says "A doctor," the rest of the class laughs and says, "You ain't gonna be nothing," or "You better hope you even get out of school." That doesn't happen in their ethnic counterpart schools. There children are encouraged. To become something is the rule, not the exception.

In our community, it's the exception who makes it out, who by some quirk of fate wanders into some alley of reinforcement and is subsequently encouraged. Until we can change and make the alley the main street, we will continue to write about the crisis, talk about the number in jail and the number not in school. The problem is deep-seated: It is psycho-emotional. It is psycho-cultural. And it will take a cultural-political effort to effect a change. Is it worth it? Of course! We are talking about our future. Either we make the effort and be men and women, or we will become history.

Many other cultures raise their children to believe that they are important and special simply because of who they *are*. Their group identity is paramount, and around that comes the family. Culture is important not just in terms of music and art; it provides a structure to help us grow and develop a sense of being and purpose, pride, character, and confidence. When the culture instills those kinds of values, it is easier to grow up with a sense of pride. The structure of black culture does not yet contain those elements that make our children feel that being black is important. This leaves them without a sense of special identity. The emphasis instead is on being an individual, and then it's the individual that becomes important, not the group. As individuals we need a leader to mold us, guide us, hold us together, pull us together to make us one—to make us function as a group. One can argue that group dynamics can cause a lower level of creativity; at the same time, it does allow for the group to work together better, as exemplified by the Muslims.

Just as an individual may be passive or aggressive, so may a people. There are certain dynamics both internal and external to a culture that can almost guarantee that most of its members will be passive. When we look at black culture, we see great passivity—the church flock who look almost blindly to their preacher for guidance; women who prostitute themselves for a controlling pimp; slaves bound in servitude to their master; the wife who is beaten by her husband yet continues to stay with him. We have created in our culture a situation in which most of our children grow up with little self-esteem. They exhibit passive, self-destructive behavior because they have been made to feel worthless. People who feel that they are nothing are prime targets for any kind of manipulator or charlatan, be it minister or pimp or sadist. An individual who is bright but passive is less likely to succeed in the world than someone who is not as bright but who has more of an aggressive personality, because the latter will naturally have more self-confidence.

This is where the home is vitally important, because it is in the home that self-confidence begins. It is in the home that children are made to feel important. This is where they should hear positive input, that they *can* do, they *will* do. They will get enough negative input from the rest of the world; hearing it also at home is destructive—it fills them with self-doubt and makes

WILBERT JORDAN

them less likely to want to take chances, to move ahead. Too many black parents are negative, and that negativity can lead to long-term deleterious consequences for their children. Instead of "You ain't nothing," "You can't do," "Don't," "Stop," kids need to hear "Yes, you can," "Go ahead," "Whatever you want to do."

If we are to effect a change, we must address this problem at its core. It is not jobs or a lack thereof. It is a lack of institutional and cultural structure; it is a basic problem in the family; and we and our culture must pay attention. We, and only we, can solve this problem. Constitutional amendments cannot; welfare has proven that it cannot. Only a people "self-healing" can—and must—do this.

On the Way

4. Testimony of a Good Nigger*

(Ba da ba ba ba babop! Ba da ba babop! Ba da ba babow!
Badeya! Badeya! Badeeya eeyaeeyaeeyaeeya!
Ba da ba babow!)

I am a *good nigger.*
There, I said it.
Said it like I'm answering the call from certain advertisements on black radio stations in L.A.

"I Need a Man!" this sister shouts with that *Sapphire* edge we can thank Hollywood for, in ads aired between oldies-but-goodies for them black plays that are wildly popular in L.A. and other big cities. Plays with names like *A Good Man Is Hard to Find, Beauty Shop, Beauty Shop 2, Mama I Want to Sing, Mama I Want to Sing 2,* and, of course, *Mama, I Need a Man Who Can Make Me Sang While I Get My Hair Did in the Beauty Shop.* These plays make money, which is why we have so many sequels, and on those ads the canned laughter busts a gut in the background. The announcer is always shouting urgently: "Back by popular demand!" or "Held over one more week!"

---

*Journalistic note in the interest of fairness: The following represents my uncensored perspective of myself, and my potential, without balancing input from my former spouses. If y'all want to know what they think, let your fingers do the walking. . . .

I mean, I've been a fly on the wall when some sisters ask wearily, "Where are all the good niggers?" Answering after only a beat: "They either in jail, gay, on dope, insane, or dating white women."

And the last two are *clearly* the same thing!

So, like the Marvalettes used to say: Here I am, baby. I'm not Sapphire's elusive *The Good Nigger,* who can melt the physical and mental bars jailing black men, *shazam!* a gay brother into Shaft, calm a mumbling streetwalker into common sense, 12-Step my man off that alcoholic steam, or untwine the fingers of a gnarly dude and his California Girl. I don't have no superpowers, and I ain't making no claims to nothing but one little thing.

I am a good man. A decent man. Good father. Good listener. Attentive lover. Literate. Humane. Honest. Straight. Sane. Drug-free. Hard-working. Funny. Don't be tripping over white women. Don't see women as property. Don't hit nobody. I cook. I'm clean. Wash dishes. Vacuum floors.

You get the picture.

Don't get me wrong, though. I'm good, but I don't mean I'm perfect. Right up front, I'll run my rap sheet:

I've been married twice and can't seem to get it right. I live apart from my two children (struggling to stay tight with them). Behind on child support. Got a stubborn streak. I'm cranky. Can't stand people swear they know me cause they read a book or seen a movie. Don't take kindly to supervision. Cuss too much. Don't go to church. Don't like shopping in malls. Tell collection agency reps to kiss my ass. Don't trust the government. Don't trust most of what I see on American TV. Oh, and I mostly would rather hear Eddie Kendricks than Charlie Parker (though I can get with Bird).

I'm trying to come clean here.

But I am a good man. Period.

I was raised right, that's the first reason. Second reason is that I work at it every day. Being and becoming is in my own hands, with help from historical and *present-tense* folk whose lives I find full of light and vitamins. I'm not unusual, if the range of cats I

PETER J. HARRIS

have met is any indication. I trust my instincts on this, since, of course, I haven't met all the good brothers on the planet, not to mention the lames.

I am not a good man because I am a male feminist or because I've been a 4.0 student of black women's invigorating contribution to America's movements (though I can get with that).

I'm a good man because I'm me and I'm happy to be me.

Ba da ba ba ba babop! Ba da ba babop! Ba da ba babow! Badeya! Badeya! Badeeya eeyaeeyaeeyaeeya! Ba da ba babow!

Make me sing like I'm an Earth, Wind & Fire song. I do hope y'all remember humming that sweet, wordless tune. It's called "Brazilian Rhyme," and it closed side one of the Fire's *All 'N All* LP. I know you know how Earth, Wind & Fire just get happy and start singing *ooooooohhhs* and *aaaaahhhs* and *eeeeeeyaaahhhs,* just cause they feel like it, stretching syllables full of heart and soul in songs full of bright horns, rhythmic stops and starts, and voices celebrating the fact of existence, voices celebrating the song just because . . . yeah, just because. . . .

Voices that are satisfied with themselves, just like I am satisfied with myself.

I ain't never apologizing for myself again. Never comparing myself to nobody else, to no person. Never again. I've accepted myself, dig myself. I'm digging into myself. I've decided to make some affirmative assumptions: If I'm cool, then so are millions of other men. If I'm struggling to stay up, then so are millions of other men. If I love, and have tried to love, black women, then so have millions of other men. If I'm on a mission to the heart of my best self, then so are millions of other men.

Ba da ba ba ba babop! Ba da ba babop! Ba da ba babow! Badeya! Badeya! Badeeya eeyaeeyaeeyaeeya! Ba da ba babow!

I'm not defensive, either. I know some brothers think misdirected ass-kicking is a badge of honor. Rather smack a daughter, son, or lover than confront their sidewalk paralysis. Rather fuck over each other than work out to the core of the problem. Rather stay up on the surface of everything than dig a tunnel to the rock that go with connecting with somebody. I ain't worried about being compared to them. Like I said, you will have some lames in the mix.

But you know what? Even them cats can change. Quickest thing that will change them is when their victims turn around and find the power and weapons to defend themselves. I'm for that. But right now, we in crisis cause of all this emotional and physical weaponry available and being used in the counterattack. So I got to find another, humane, way to help change a brother for the better. I'm for that. I still believe the best way to change somebody for good, to change them to do good for the rest of their life, is to inspire them to change.

I'll tell you why after this quote from a novel called *The Healers* by Ayi Kwei Armah:

> The healer devotes himself to inspiration. He also lives against manipulation. [Manipulation is] a disease, a popular one. It comes from spiritual blindness. If I'm not spiritually blind, I see your spirit. I speak to it if I want to invite you to do something with me. If your spirit agrees it moves your body and your body acts. That's inspiration. But if I'm blind to your spirit I see only your body. Then if I want you to do something for me I force or trick your body into doing it even against your spirit's direction. That's manipulation. Manipulation steals a person's body from his spirit, cuts the body off from its own spirit's direction. The healer is a lifelong enemy of all manipulation. The healer's method is inspiration. (Nairobi: East African Publishing House, 1978, p. 99)

All right, I'm busted. I'm really *not* a good nigger.
I'm a healer.

There, I've said it. Said it in the sympathetic voice you can thank black churches for. That voice you hear within the harmony when the Fire's Maurice White and Philip Bailey offi-

PETER J. HARRIS

cially snatch a love song into a realm way beyond the charts. Full of understanding and hope, and any laughter is live and mutual and it ain't in the background. This is the historical voice that's given even the most exasperated sister energy to climb over the weariness because she believes in our goodness.

I'm a healer. Not the elusive *The Healer.* Just one healer against manipulation and for inspiration. Believing black men have the capacity to act and do right. Resting on our tradition of contribution above and beyond any definition that describes us only as reflections of male privilege.

I want to communicate with black men. I want to encourage them to be their best selves. I want to heal their wounds. I have high expectations of black men. My calling card is the benefit of the doubt. I am not trying to be an expert or spokesman for black men. I see black men as experts on their own lives. I humbly ask them what's on their minds. I listen. I risk trust. I believe if I come at brothers cleanly, they will respond cleanly. My experience says with common sense and common courtesy, we can short-circuit a lot of defensiveness and belligerence just below the surface in some brothers. My experience says passionate and persistent common sense and common courtesy are actually political styles that counterattack America's historical breakdown on black men.

Reminds me of how all them bowtie-wearing cats out the Nation of Islam always call you "Sir" when they pushing their papers and pies. I've even been asked if I was Muslim because I am quick to call a cat "Sir" in public. I been in Muslim businesses in cities across America, and the men and women who work there never fail to address me as "Sir." It's contagious. No, I'm not a Muslim, have no desire to convert to Islam, and I'm not here to debate their philosophy. I'm simply telling you that whenever I'm in public, especially when I'm in public, I'm quick to call a black man "Sir"—whether he's panhandling that quarter on city streets, standing with me in the supermarket line, or balling with me on the basketball court.

Testimony of a Good Nigger

And the *normal* reaction is for them to be cool in return. In other words, the *human* response is to be cool. Defenses melt. Cats be smiling. Courtesy is the rule. Maybe it's my unapologetic leap of faith to think—no, *feel*—this is a foundation from which we can help black men heal their psychic and social wounds. Maybe it's my own brand of street corner philosophy to believe treating a man like a human being will mean, nine times out of ten, getting treated like one in return. Maybe there ain't enough science in my argument for the real experts to take it seriously.

Well, just who are the experts on black men?

Who's able to spread on the table facts and figures, evidence and analysis, examples and anecdotes, songs and stories that say there is no room for an effective, national surge of common courtesy, mutual respect, healing laughter, intelligent challenge, intense listening, and downright kindness toward every black man we come to meet?

Who's got the magic words, government study, or Bible printout that documents some alternative formula we need to excite a man into reaching his potential? Who's throwing out the first pitch on the seventh game which will determine Mr. October of the heart and soul?

Ba da ba ba ba babop! Ba da ba babop! Ba da ba babow! Badeya! Badeya! Badeeya eeyaeeyaeeyaeeya! Ba da ba babow!

I got somebody for you. 5th Street Dick. Real name Richard Fulton, owner of 5th St. Dick's Coffee Co., a cafe and jazz club in L.A.'s Crenshaw neighborhood called Leimert Park, where Fulton and other committed men and women operate businesses that cater to the soul as much as the bottom line. Leimert Park is full of "arts businesses," such as galleries, music stores and stages, shops that sell African clothes, black books, and cobbler (that's right, *cobbler!*). The square-block area is anchored by Marla Gibbs's arts education complex and 1,100-seat theater.

PETER J. HARRIS

For my money, though, 5th Street Dick is the flesh-and-blood prism of Leimert Park. Through him the decay and potential of a human being, especially an African American man, has been absorbed and converted into a life that splashes inspiration in all directions, especially onto Higher Ground. His life—*success on a sidewalk scale*—reflects individual desire and collective encouragement.

He was named by Homeless Homies after the downtown L.A. street he slept on for four years in the mid-'70s, when he was hooked on Windsor Canadian (or whatever poison he could cop with whatever change he could cop). Fulton still calls himself a "tramp." Not entrepreneur, even though his club has been open since the spring of 1992 (days before L.A. exploded after the Rodney King verdicts in Simi Valley, in fact) and has become one of *the* places to go to hear live jazz, sip some coffee, and be hip without showing out.

On the fall Saturday afternoon he talks about his life, Fulton sits out front of his cafe on 43rd Place, nurses a cup of coffee, smokes Café Crème cigars, and greets folks walking past or easing in and out the cafe to the rhythm of a group called Blues Underground, featuring singer Roy Jones. He wears blue jeans and a black T-shirt sporting white lettering that says "Watts [after the seminal L.A. 'hood] University."

"I come from a good family," he says quietly, talking about a journey from his home in Pittsburgh to the streets of Los Angeles. An early East Coast leg of his trip included transfer to an all-white high school in Pittsburgh. Followed by a Marine Corps tour of 'Nam. In 1975, after discharge in Washington, D.C., he drove to L.A.

Four months after he got out of the service, he was on the streets, Fulton says.

How did he become homeless?

Fulton offers no straight answer, only this sketch of his childhood and youth:

"I don't know. My father was always working. He was never home. But I had everything I ever wanted. I was sucked out of

Testimony of a Good Nigger

the black area to a white school. I started to go the other way because of rebellion. . . ." He sighs. "I think it's important to let a child know that it's wonderful being black. I think it's important to tell *brothers* how it's wonderful being black. It took me fifty years to understand that.

"I run this whole thing on that," he says, pointing to the cafe. "I'm not a miracle worker. I'm exactly what you see. I'm a tramp. I don't manage money well. I don't pay my bills [on time every month]. But I get that [respect] from the people who come here. In turn, I can give you that."

"It wasn't alcohol that led to downtown L.A.'s canyons," he says emphatically. "It was me!" Ironically, he says, "If it wasn't for alcohol, I probably wouldn't be alive."

Alcohol led him to Alcoholics Anonymous meetings at the Crenshaw Alano Club, located on Leimert Boulevard, around the corner from where he eventually opened his cafe. "Over a period of time, I didn't want to drink anymore. I didn't think I could survive drinking anymore. AA allowed me time in between not having a drink. The more time I stayed there, the more I stayed away from drink."

He's been sober since 1979. Every day, he spends time at the Crenshaw Alano Club with people he calls friends. His life has convinced Fulton that basic and genuine communication is "the most important thing" in connecting people. And connection is the key to reaching human potential.

"When I was on skid row, I was devoid of people. I was isolated and I was an isolationist. Being without people, you can't get no information to help yourself. Oh, you shuffle through a lot of things . . . blood banks . . . but you're not there. Some people treated me kind. I didn't think nobody was treating me right, let alone myself. But if they would come and talk to you, even if they told you about you doing something bad, that let you know they cared about you.

"Most people looked at you as if you don't exist, as if you're not there. Some people were kind to me. That made me feel

PETER J. HARRIS

good. That's the most important thing. That's like the most you can do for another person, regardless of race or creed. It's the most important thing you can do. Speaking, saying hello. Continue to speak. You're acknowledging that they're alive."

As Fulton speaks, a homeless man who couldn't be out of his twenties walks past with a sack slung over his shoulder. The man cracks intensely that Fulton didn't show him respect during an earlier meeting. Fulton loudly answers, "Well, I'm sorry" to the black man, who's walking fast. The man pauses long enough to hear Fulton continue: "I didn't mean no harm. I'm just protecting my thing, but I ain't trying to step on yours." The man could have been the model for the logo Fulton has painted on his cafe sign—a "tramp" pushing a shopping cart full of cans. He tilts his head to digest Fulton's explanation, then accepts it with a nod OK. The man throws up an open hand, hitches his bag, and walks off.

"You have to be open to know people," 5th Street Dick says. "All people got that innate ability to know when somebody is speaking honestly and that they care. That's *got* to be a natural thing. Animosity, hate, all that is a *taught* thing. I don't make no presumptions. I just speak. I tell you what I'll do: I allow you to give me an idea who you are. I don't want to impose my judgments on how you are. I observe. I watch. I speak. I try to keep my word . . . I try to keep my word as close as possible.

"You know what I really try to do? Speak to the kids who come in with their parents. I think it's really important to speak to the male child. We're afraid of our young kids. We have allowed everybody in the world to make our kids monsters. Our kids are nothing but kids. We hide from them.

"The world really is a strain on you, especially a black male. To get up and deal with this chaotic, misinformed, misdirected world we got to live in . . . where at any moment you can get shot, locked up, and they don't give a damn if you got a white collar and driving a Mercedes. . . . To get up and roll on that. . . ."

He shakes his head.

Testimony of a Good Nigger

"If I went to skid row tomorrow, I'd go with another philoso-phy. It would never be the same. Only thing that would make it the same is if I started drinking again. Now I know I'm OK. And the more OK I get with myself, the more OK the whole world gets. Everybody—those I know and those I don't know, everybody I see every day and those I see only once in my life-time—they *all* became important."

What 5th Street Dick says may not be science, but it's got a ring of hard-won truth to it.

The healers are out here, y'all.

We got to see them, though, for who they are. Respect their different styles. We got to create a personal and social atmo-sphere and institution in which our styles can be seen and felt without flinching. Flinching before a cat can even gather his thoughts to tell you how his style can contribute to problem solving or community building. We got to free up the consider-ation and respect for black men's sincere emotional and intellec-tual perspectives the same way we say, "Oh yeah," and pay money for the undisputed wizardry of some of our entertain-ment geniuses.

See, that socially accepted wizardry is really a distilled reflec-tion of our emotional and intellectual gifts.

Let's *Moonwalk* into the realm of black men as equal partners whose sense of mission, compassion, and commitment are natu-ral resources that can benefit all of us. Let's *slamdunk* all precon-ceptions about a black man based on what the media say, or our individual bad experiences, and open ourselves to the possibility that the next brother got something nourishing to offer. Let's *work the audience* like any good stand-up comic does, by listen-ing, observing, and improvising. Come to the gig with a pol-ished wit and prepared for hecklers, no question, but always ready to roll with the flow to make that contact which raises the stakes, opens up people's minds, and results in call and response.

So, like, this is the unscientific, Richard Fulton–tested for-

PETER J. HARRIS

mula for helping find that good man and unleashing the healer in all of us:

Accepting black male humanity, cultivating black male humanity, insisting on black male humanity, demanding black male humanity, celebrating black male humanity. Listening for and hearing the accented voices—the *Badeya! Badeya! Badeeya eeyaeeyaeeyaeeya!*—echoing in the hearts of black men. The voices that inspire black men. The voices of inspired black men. The voices that unlock the code for goodness in black men.

As for me, every day I'm risking field tests of this formula, filtering it through my own style. I meet new cats with an open heart, a challenging sense of manhood. I welcome their ideas. Respect their opinions. I listen. I agree. I disagree. I compromise. I laugh. I let live. I live.

If somebody can bust my formula, come on with it! But here's the real test of any strategy to claim and incorporate the best we are, far as I'm concerned:

Do black men have a real chance of speaking for themselves, describing the world in their honest, original ways, to the depths of their deepest breaths? Is it my voice speaking for me? Because if I'm spoken for by even a *New Jack* Interlocutor—man or woman—it's bogus.

Any good nigger can see that.

And a healer can *X-Ray* it!

Ba da ba ba ba babop! Ba da ba babop! Ba da ba babow! Badeya! Badeya! Badeeya eeyaeeyaeeyaeeya! Ba da ba babow!

Ad lib to fade

Wounded Man

5. Voodoo for Charles

On Christmas morning in 1991 I telephoned my nephew. I have two nephews: Charles, who had only just turned nineteen the week before, and Wayne, Jr., who is somewhere in his middle twenties by now. These are the children of my brother's first marriage. My nephews grew up in Newark, New Jersey, where much of my early childhood was spent, but that was before the conflagration of the 1967 riot and the razing of what remained of the city by the local, state, and federal governments in the name of an urban renewal which is yet to come. While Newark was not an easy city to live in, it was still, in any case, from the late fifties to the mid-sixties (when I lived there with my great-grandmother in the black district called the Hill) a city. Today Newark is the ghost of a city. Its statistics for AIDS, black-on-black crime, infant mortality, and unemployment bear witness to dissolution.

Charles was living in Newark in 1991. I had not spoken to him in more than four years. I hadn't seen him in a longer time. The last time we'd spoken was by telephone. (For several years now, I seem to talk to the members of my family only on the phone.) By 1991 I still felt unresolved about our last conversation. I had been visiting my parents' house in Philadelphia, while they were away on a trip. "Uncle Don," Charles had said to me on the phone back then, "where's Grandad and Gramma? I want to tell them I got shot."

His father had divorced his mother when Charles was six. My brother had married again after renouncing the street life he'd embraced almost his entire youth. His second marriage was to a middle-class black woman nine years younger than he (and one year younger than I). She was a preacher's daughter. My brother soon became an evangelical preacher himself. Since my brother has renounced what he often calls, from the pulpit, the sin and shame of his former life, he has also, tragically, renounced his sons. He is uncomfortable with them. It is as if they are his doubles. They *are* him, but with a frightening difference. They are projections of all the parts of himself that he has disowned in order to achieve his new life. They still know little more than the brutal reality of the streets he fled. They also remember him as the junkie who beat their mother, and they still bear the mental and spiritual wounds of that. He does not talk to them, any more than our father spoke to him, because to talk to them might mean confronting the past from which he is always running; it might mean allowing that past into his present. Instead, he quotes the self-hating apostle Paul when I criticize his abandonment of his sons, proclaiming himself a new creature in Christ. "All old things," he assures me, parroting Saint Paul, "are passed away." My brother now has three young daughters with his new wife. When his new wife was pregnant with the last girl, she called me on the phone and said, "Your brother wants a boy, but I pray it's another girl. It's easier for black girls than it is for black boys."

In the four years since I'd spoken to Charles, his mother had been murdered in the housing project where both she and her children were raised. Had it been easier for her? After having been shot (almost fatally, for refusing to run drugs for a neighborhood syndicate), Charles recovered and began his career as a drug lord in Newark. Recently he had been sentenced to three to seven years in prison for attempted murder, a sentence from which he was on the lam on Christmas, 1991. He was *nineteen.*

The phone rang several times before there was an answer at the number that another relative had provided. The voice that

DON BELTON

answered was a man's, husky, low. I wondered if this was the new voice, the man's voice, of the mercurial black baby boy whom I'd helped to raise. I asked if Charles was there.

"Who is this?" the voice asked, gruff.

"I'm sorry," I said. I'd been told he was in hiding. "This is his uncle, Don."

"Uncle Don?" I listened to the voice come alive, filling with pleasure, softening, turning into a boy's. "Uncle Don?"

Suddenly I was afraid, awed by the power of the telephone to create the illusion that pushing a sequence of buttons was all that was required for me to reach Charles. He was, after all, now speaking into my ear—this was his voice; we had each other on the line. I also felt regret that it had taken me so long to complete such a simple action.

He wanted to know where I was calling from. He said he'd heard I lived in Maine. I told him I live in Saint Paul, Minnesota.

"Minneapolis?" he asked. "Where Prince lives?"

"Yes."

He told me he'd seen the book I'd written, at his great-aunt's house in Newark. He said he wanted to read it. I promised to send him a copy. I told him I was writing another, a section of which I had dedicated to the memory of his mother when it was published in a literary journal. I don't really know much that is certain about his mother, though I knew her, except that she was mellow-voiced and pretty when she was young. Her skin was the color of yellowed ivory, she had freckles, and her name was the same as my own mother's.

"You're a teacher, aren't you? At a college?"

"Yes," I said. "I teach literature."

I wonder what Charles thinks of my life. I know he's been told I am a success, though I doubt he understands why. I doubt he knows mine is a success I sometimes can barely feel, though I live in a multicultural (predominantly white, middle-class) neighborhood, where my white heterosexual neighbors tolerate my homosexuality, my blackness, my intellectual bent. A num-

Voodoo for Charles

ber of the neighbors have adopted children of color from the American South, Peru, Korea. Others are busy making babies. The parents accept me ostensibly, but they make certain I never babysit. I wanted to tell Charles I'm gay. I came out to most of the adults in my family years ago. I wanted him to learn from me that his uncle loves men.

I also wanted to tell him what it has been like for me teaching at a college whose faculty I joined in 1990, a college that has failed to tenure a single black professor in twenty years, about the stress of sometimes confronting a racism so covert and insidious that our ancestors could not have imagined it. I wanted to tell him that although I was preparing a lecture that I would give in a few weeks in Paris at the Sorbonne, my life felt permeated by a soul-sick sadness I inherited from my father and my father's father (both of whom were named Charles) and share with my nephew's father. Obviously Charles is a part of this, and I believed that if I could discuss this sadness with Charles (surely he was now old enough for this conversation), could share my names for it with him and hear the names he gave to it, then we might touch that hurt together and help each other heal. But something prevented me. I wasn't afraid that he would cease to look up to me if he knew my life isn't the magazine of success our relatives want to pretend it is; I was afraid of the incoherence that stretched out before me when I thought of naming the pain we were both a part of. Any words I might speak would have to be words used in faith, since I did not know their exact power to hurt or heal. To speak them I would have to trust myself and trust Charles, trust love. And I was unable to speak those words of faith that morning.

I did the best I could. I opened the door as wide as I could to my nephew, hoping he might, because of his youth or his reck-lessness, push it further. "So how are things with you?" I asked him. "I haven't seen you in so long. Talk to me."

I listened as my nephew brought me up to date on his life with the same adolescent mixture of nonchalance, anxiety, and

DON BELTON

wonder with which I had once reported to my parents about a backpack trip to Quebec City in 1975, life in my college dorm, or meeting James Baldwin at his brother David's apartment on Manhattan's West Side when I was a sophomore.

Trying to listen beneath my nephew's words for his feelings—for his life and my own—my mind wandered over all I already knew of Charles's life. He had been out of my life for so long, and, more important—since he had once been in part my responsibility—I had been out of his. I wondered if I would even recognize my nephew were I to pass him by chance on the street in my city, or see his face in a video clip accompanying the all too familiar TV news narration about another anonymous (even when named) young black male criminal murdered, imprisoned, standing trial, beaten.

I thought about the times when my nephews were little. Even though I was only thirteen when Wayne, Jr., was born and sixteen when Charles was born, I took my role as their uncle quite seriously. My brother had become a junkie shortly after Wayne, Jr., was born, and though he was clean when Charles was conceived, he'd begun using again before Charles was delivered. Between the births of my nephews, my star had begun to ascend. I received an academic scholarship to an exclusive Quaker boys' school in Philadelphia. Education, it seemed, was the sword I could use to vanquish racism. If I hewed to the assimilationist line, studied and got good grades, dressed and spoke properly, went to church, I would become something better than a criminal or a corpse. I soon tried to pass these values on to my nephews—even though I had begun to feel a certain amount of ambivalence, distance, and irony in relation to these values even then. I knew instinctively from the moment I first saw my nephews that they were born into a world full of trouble.

I used to take them everywhere with me whenever I could be with them. I dragged them to the library, bookstores, plays. I remember, later, the train trips down from my exclusive New

Voodoo for Charles

England college, arriving at Newark station—a monstrosity always under construction and restoration, a sad remnant of the populuxe shrine to mobility I'd traveled through when I was a child, the times I shuttled back and forth between Philadelphia and Newark, between belligerently bourgeois parents and my Southern immigrant great-grandmother, a hickory-skinned crone with long puff-of-smoke hair.

When I took the train down for my nephews, it was invariably a trial to find a cab driver—black or white—willing to transport me to the notorious housing project where my nephews lived. I remember walking up stinking stairways and through dark hallways to find their apartment, sometimes finding their mother high on drugs with her boyfriend and her sister, or finding no one at home at all.

"Oh, Uncle Don," Charles was saying on Christmas morning in 1991, "did I tell you Aunt Geraldine died of AIDS?"

I remember searching the grounds of the project when no one was home, and finding Wayne and Charles in some glass-strewn play yard amid the wild bedlam of unsupervised children—unsupervised except for the foxlike vigil of men and women whose preying on children takes various forms, all deadly. I would take my nephews to a friend's place in the country or to the city, to a planetarium, a museum, a movie, a historical site, *any*place that said to them there *is* someplace—some *way*—other than this.

By the time I moved from college to graduate school, I was spending more time with Charles because he was still young enough to be at home, while Wayne, Jr., grew harder to locate during my visits. Wayne, Jr., was running with a bad crowd, picking up the legacy his father had escaped and left for him in Newark's streets. When I did see my oldest nephew, I realized that in my absence he was rapidly becoming a man I didn't understand. (This was before the violent, misanthropic music he now favored and the disaffected style of dress he'd adopted were appropriated and commodified by the white media.)

DON BELTON

I was worried about Wayne, Jr., increasingly unsure with him now that he was becoming a man. I went back and forth, reaching out to him and hoping he would reach out to me. I worried that it might not be good for him to spend too much time with me anymore, that I knew too little about that street world in which he was striving. I knew that though I'd come from Newark, the destruction waiting in its streets had not remained the same. It had metastasized. In that world he would have been my mentor. I might encourage his tenderness, and that might be his undoing in that world. I couldn't give him what he needed to survive there. He knew that. I hoped to share with him some of what he might need to get out. If he wanted it. And I'd hoped to give him that from the first time I carried him across a room.

But Charles was still a child. He clearly needed me. I struggled to give him everything I'd given his brother too late, the experience of being prized. It had been an experience I'd somehow created or been given, perhaps by my great-grand-mother, in my own early childhood. My storytelling, "part-Indian" great-grandmother with the smokecloud hair was my primary caregiver off and on from my birth until I was nine years old. She chose me, chose me to invest with her stories and accu-mulated legacy, which is to say she loved me. With Charles I was in a hurry, because I knew that the world I left him in every time I returned him to his mother's apartment was a world in which children became old abruptly, without warning.

I told him the same stories I'd taught his brother. I told him about his great-great-grandfather on my mother's side, who moved his wife and children all over South Carolina before he came to Philadelphia around the turn of the century, always a step ahead of the Klan, because he refused to accept the large and small indignities white men meted out to colored men. In Saluta, South Carolina, he'd been the first black man to attend the auction of cotton he raised on his homestead, not because he was granted special permission but because he demanded a basic

Voodoo for Charles

right. In Philadelphia he had a "contract" with movie princess Grace Kelly's father, John B. Kelly, the brick magnate, to supply the work crews for building operations, though I cannot imagine what a contract between a black man and an Irishman looked like in the early nineteen-tens. He moved his family into a big house in the once-progressive neighborhood near Girard College in North Philadelphia.

I once took Charles to the ruin of this house, near Girard Avenue. We stood at the entrance and called our ancestor's name. We could see from the entrance to the backyard. A tree was growing through the kitchen into the second floor. For a time Great-Grandfather had rented the house next door to help an ongoing chain of relatives from the South relocate and find work. He lost his mind after the unionization of his trade empowered newly arrived white ethnics and ousted black men from the professions of carpentry and masonry. My mother grew up with him living on the third floor of her family home, a withdrawn, bitter old man who occasionally came to life when he took his fiddle down from the mantle and ordered his grandchildren to dance until they went crying to their mother, "Please, make Grand-Pop behave!"

Charles learned old songs from my collection of reissued recordings by Louis Armstrong, Bessie Smith, Cab Calloway, Ethel Waters. There was one Waters song that always broke him up; it had the spoken line *Take it easy, greasy, . . . you got a long way to slide.* Charles loved singing and language. He was a miraculous dark bird when he was little, always echoing and articulating. Before he turned two he had a good command of adjectives and adverbs. He was always narrating his experience. I am told that small children usually exhibit exceptional verbal skills or advanced physical skills early. Charles exhibited both. He loved to run and climb and dance. He was fondest of his push toys. When he was four or five, I bought him toy boxing gloves and we practiced his jabs and footwork. I'd make the sound of the opening bell and he would start bobbing, weaving, and hooking.

DON BELTON

He had the classic combination down pat: the left jab followed by the right cross. I called him Kid Chocolate, after the legendary 1920s black boxer. I used to tell him his boxing technique was pure voodoo.

Charles was my heart. I was his uncle, almost his father, even if only for the day, the weekend, the week or summer we were together.

Once Charles fell riding his tricycle and split his tongue. I rushed him to the hospital emergency room and had to curse out the receptionist before he was admitted. "We can't admit him without the consent of his parent—that means a mother or father," the receptionist had told me from a barred cage. I was standing there with Charles's blood drenching my polo shirt. "*I'm* his goddamned parent!" I railed. "What's it to you? What kind of shit is this?"

I believe I am being objective when I say Charles was the most beautiful baby I have ever seen, more beautiful than his brother, who was perfect, and, if pictures are any indication, more beautiful than his father or I had been. His skin was darker than ours at the same time that it was more brilliant. He shone. His was a preternatural blackness dedicated to the light. His round face was like a thundercloud with the lightning of his eyes and teeth flashing constantly inside it. Charles was the resurrected promise of all our childhoods going back generations for our manhood. I loved that boy better than my life. He *was* my life. Only better. Even before he was born, I was always talking to him, reading to him. When his mother was pregnant with him, I used to sit by her and touch her stomach and read to him inside her womb. I read him James Baldwin's letter to his nephew from *The Fire Next Time:* "You can only be destroyed by believing that you really are what the white world calls a *nigger.* I tell you this because I love you, and please don't you ever forget it."

But as I've said, by the time Charles was born, his father was back on heroin. My brother tried many times to save himself, to

Voodoo for Charles

heal, to redeem himself, and no one knows better than I do that he was born into a world of trouble. And maybe the reason I loved his sons so much was that I loved my brother, and I hoped I could redeem him if I could help redeem them.

*

The following is one of my earliest memories. It emanates from both my memory and my imagination. It is literally true; however, in terms of the organic infrastructure informing my life, it has the quality of supertruth. Once, when I was four and staying in Philadelphia for the summer, my brother and I were walking home from Sunday school. The afternoon was sultry-hot. We were in no hurry to get home. I held his hand, as I always did when we walked down the street together, and he swung our arms in a jovial way. Soon we heard thunder and saw the zigzag lightning. The swinging of my arm slowed. As we walked, we were caught in the downpour.

The rain pounded so hard it hurt my small body. I had never been outside in weather like that, away from home, in the street, without my mother or my father. All I had was my brother to protect me. He was lanky, athletic, almost as tall as my father. We began to run. The rain poured like a mirror of heaven. My brother held my hand tight. Lightning flashed, thunder rumbled, and I began to scream and cry.

I stopped running, and my brother stopped. I couldn't move. I was too terrified. I believed I would die. God was angry. He was tearing up the world and washing it away. I fully realize now what I realized then only in part, that my brave fourteen-year-old brother was terrified too. But he said, "It's all right. I'm with you. I'll get you home." This vow was punctuated by a burst of thunder so loud it threatened to crack open the street before us. My brother took me and ran first in one direction and then another. We rushed along the flowing curb. Then we were standing near a tree. We had reached the elementary school building two blocks from our house.

DON BELTON

"We're almost there," my brother shouted over the ringing wind. "Do you want me to carry you?"

"No," I said, "I'm scared."

"All right," he told me. "We'll rest for a little while."

We ran from the tree to the awning leading into the school building. As soon as we came up against the closed glass entrance, there was a big burst of lightning. For an instant the world went white. The skin of my neck and arms tingled. We held each other. I felt his heart leaping just above my head, but he held me, and I didn't cry. We stood there holding each other until the rain slowed. Then we walked home in silence.

My father was sitting in the living room, reading the newspaper. My mother came out from the kitchen. I was excited. I wanted to tell them how my brother had saved me from the storm and brought me home safe like he promised. "You better take off those wet things," my mother said immediately. "Go on upstairs." As we turned on the stairs, my father said that my brother should leave his clothes off when he removed the wet things and remain upstairs in the bathroom. He said that he'd received a call from church, that Wayne had stolen money from the Sunday school collection. My father had also found money missing from the coin collection he kept hidden in our basement. He was going to whip my brother.

The terror I'd felt in the storm returned. My father was a strong but soft-spoken man. I waited in the bathroom with my brother until our father came in with the piece of ironing cord. Wayne and I had been sitting on the rim of the bathtub. He was naked except for his blue jockey shorts. I had dressed myself in my Daniel Boone outfit. I held my brother's hands, telling him not to worry. His saffron body was still marked from the last beating he'd received from our father that summer.

Our father put me out, but I turned and stood at the door. I could see him through the slightly opened door, lashing my brother's legs and back with the cord. At first Wayne fought back, and my father lost his balance for a moment near the sink. He righted himself and bore down on my brother, muttering

Voodoo for Charles

and striking him, lashing him into the floor with the ironing cord. I ran downstairs to my mother in the kitchen. I told her to call the police. I said Daddy was killing Wayne. She did not move. Had she ceased to be our mother? It was a long time that we stood in the kitchen, listening to the lashing and crying upstairs, before she said flatly, "He's got to learn. Your father is beating him because he loves him. He's beating him so the police won't have to."

*

The last time I saw my nephew Charles, he was fourteen or fifteen years old. I had taken him to lunch at a restaurant inside the John Wanamaker department store, a historic illustrated text of upward mobility in downtown Philadelphia. I had been told by his mother that he was having trouble in school. This was nothing new. From the time Charles began school, though he entered able to read, write, count, multiply, and divide, he was labeled a problem child by teachers who were either unwilling or unable to address the accelerated needs of a child like him in an overcrowded Newark classroom.

At Wanamaker's, I talked to him about school, which he thoroughly hated by then, and about his young life, which he was coming to hate as well. As I listened to him, I could hear that he had already arrived at his youth's end. His voice grumbled with loss.

"Listen here, Kid Chocolate," I said, about to launch into my "value of education" talk.

"Don't call me that," he pleaded. "I hate my color. I hate it. I wish I was light-skinned like you, Uncle Don."

"Baby. Man," I said, "first of all, your uncle is *not* light-skinned," and I laughed (*how could I?*), "and even if I were, you're beautiful, man. You've always been beautiful."

But he wouldn't laugh. Not even for me. I think he even hated me a little that afternoon for trying to turn the light on his

DON BELTON

dark brilliance, since to be conspicuous by one's brilliance in the world to which he was always returned was only, to him, another liability.

I should have shaken him right in that restaurant in the bright, white department store. I should have shaken him. Held him. Rocked him. I should have told him what my great-grandmother told me in one way or another every day we were together: "*You're* the one the ancestors prayed for. *You're* all our hope." I should have told Charles, "You're the one. It belongs to you. You can't give up. You better win. Remember the Kid. Kid Chocolate. Knock that mean shit out. Where's your footwork, baby? Weave. Let me see your combination. Where's that spooky jab-hook-jab? Where's your voodoo?"

But I could see that the enemies of my nephews and me knew how to manufacture the antidote to our voodoo and were now able to kill a black man-child's spirit early—and the work had already been accomplished in Charles. It was harder and harder for a black boy in Newark to slip through the system as I had done—which is not at all to suggest that my passage had been an easy one or that this nation sets no other snares for young black men besides ghettos.

Four years later, on Christmas morning in 1991, Charles was living with a thirty-year-old woman, waiting for his first child to be born. "As soon as the baby is born," he was telling me, "I'm going to turn myself in. I can do three years stiff. I'm not saying it's going to be all that easy, Uncle Don, but I can do it. Most of my friends from around the way are already in prison anyway."

"Guess what," he said, after I told him I loved him, that I believed he could still turn his life around, though I had no idea what I was talking about. I think I was in a mildly shocked state. I'd been hearing my own voice speaking to Charles as if from a distance.

"Guess what," Charles said again with a cheerfulness that finally undid me. "Now in Newark they even have surveillance cameras in the streetlights."

We both realized it at the same moment: He was already in prison. He's been in prison most of his life. And because he, my heart, is in prison, so am I.

When he hung up, I turned off the telephone. I sat in the house until it was dark, listening to records. Jelly Roll Morton. Marvin Gaye. Wayne Shorter. Sam Cooke. The Soul Stirrers. Albert Ayler. Jackie Wilson. Dexter Gordon. It was as though through the voices of these black male artists I was calling a phalanx of ancestors to rise and protect my nephew. In the evening I made a light meal. I had planned to attend a dinner party. I plugged in the telephone long enough to excuse myself. "I'm fine," I assured my hosts. I said "Merry Christmas," and my hosts and I made plans to get together "soon."

Next, I cleaned my house. I swept dust from corners. I moved furniture, sweeping. I got on my knees and scrubbed the floors in the kitchen and the bathroom. I put clothes I no longer wore away in boxes, ready for the next week's trash collection. I did the wash and changed my bed. When I was done, I felt better. I got into bed and fell into a hard sleep.

I awoke when it was still dark, the sheet and blanket twisted around my torso. In my sleep I had been dreaming and conjuring. I had awakened myself shouting, *"I'll get you home."*

DON BELTON

The Workshop

6. Singular Voice, Several Sounds

The following are thoughts on education, discipline, and music with implications for black males. The three titled excerpts are speech transcripts and an essay developed by Ellis Marsalis. The two interview excerpts are from a longer interview conducted in Elkhart, Indiana.

CULTURAL DIVERSITY

School as we know it is doomed. And every attempt to improve—but fundamentally preserve—the present system will only prolong its death throes and add immeasurably to its costs, both financial and social. By the year 2010, if we are to survive as a democratic society, our children will have to learn in a variety of new ways, some of them already on the drawing board, some unforeseen. None of them will involve a teacher in the front of a classroom presenting information to twenty or thirty children seated at desks.

This is a quote from an article in the May 1992 *Atlantic Monthly* which presents an analysis of where we are as opposed to where we should be. This commentary presents what may seem like alternatives but are really imperatives. The present makeup of the American social, political, and economic landscape demands the systematic inclusion of all its citizens. There are very few approaches toward solving the myriad problems we face as a nation of ethnics. I hope to address probable solutions in the future.

I have just completed my third year as director of Jazz Studies at the University of New Orleans. During this brief tenure, I have seen the results of sustaining a Eurocentric music curriculum in a city whose cultural milieu dictates other priorities. A declining enrollment in university music programs tends to reflect more than shrinking budgets for financial aid. If we are to stem the tide of attrition, there must be options well beyond the concert stage and the opera house. Music educators must willingly shed the cloak of conservatism to provide the necessary leadership toward culturally diverse teaching and performing. Unfortunately, cultural diversity is a concept still struggling for acceptance in a nation that likes to think of itself as culturally diverse.

As a university professor whose task it is to "teach jazz," I find it incumbent upon me to establish in my own mind just what it is I am doing in the name of teaching as well as in the name of jazz. Numerous individuals have tried to define jazz without much success. Perhaps all music exists to express feelings, emotions, attitudes that words cannot convey. Then there is the omnipresent aspect of improvisation—the impromptu actions of an instrumentalist or singer in a universe of chords and rhythms that mysteriously seem to gel at just the right moments to create sounds of joy, sorrow, surprise, ecstasy, and other emotional responses that span the myriad moods of the human personality. There is, however, a significant hurdle to cross when one attempts to organize the concepts of jazz improvisation into an academic discipline that will function within the framework of a traditional Eurocentric-based curriculum.

The Eurocentric-based curriculum establishes the rules and guidelines that are essential to the definition (both connotative

ELLIS MARSALIS

and denotative) of American culture. In an essay in an early issue of *Reconstruction*, author John Gennari commented on the state of jazz in America. "When one turned to the *New York Times*," Gennari wrote, "one found an editorial distinction between `Music' and `Jazz/Pop'—a cultural pecking order in which the Philharmonic always and forever stands higher than the World Saxophone Quartet, in which the Juilliard String Quartet is assumed to operate at a higher level of musical expression than the Modern Jazz Quartet."

This form of cultural arrogance helps to perpetuate the miseducation of our future music educators and their academic peers as well. Listening to jazz as an aesthetic experience is not germane to mainstream American sensibilities. Just as it is "possible for (John) Dizzy Gillespie to receive a Grammy 'Lifetime Achievement' Award, it is also possible for the people who gave him the award to remain unfamiliar with any particular Gillespie recording." A close observation of the systematic exclusion of jazz instruction (from the point of view of the oral tradition) graphically illustrates cultural negligence on the part of those in positions of authority.

As the twenty-first century rapidly approaches, we must be willing to embrace the reality of America as a pluralistic society, as opposed to the incontestable dominance of Eurocentricity throughout most of the twentieth century. A restructured curriculum, K through 12, must be developed to prepare students to think, reason, write, compute, and include creative activities that assist in their development of a world view as opposed to a view of the world. As I see it, education is the process of directing students toward information that will assist them in negotiating the circumstances of their environmental situation. These negotiations should be practical as well as philosophical. A university's function should not, indeed cannot, entail compensating for ill-prepared entry-level students. We are consistently developing a nation of people whose view of the world is slanted because of disinformation and misinformation.

What, then, should be the role of the university? Can a "moving society" that is constantly driven by technological developments and bottom-line mentality survive the destructiveness of one-dimensional Eurocentric thinking? Perhaps. But should not we as a nation aspire far beyond the level of mere survival? How much should we continue to sacrifice to maintain the status quo?

There are two concepts we must distinguish that are too often expressed as interchangeable entities: *certification* and *education*. As a youth I was constantly encouraged to go to college and get a degree so that I would have something to "fall back on." Therefore, the concept of becoming certified for a job took precedence over becoming educated. Certification implied doing whatever it took to get the degree, which often included blind obedience, tests on Fridays, avoidance of controversy, and prompt payment of tuition fees. Education implied development of research skills, questioning accepted beliefs and practices, and very often challenging authority figures, as well as prompt payment of tuition fees. At the university level, the demand for recruitment and retention too often causes faculty to adopt the line of least resistance to keep numbers high. Hence, education sometimes takes a back seat to certification. This practice has produced a large body of teachers/administrators in our public schools who are continually falling back-(wards) on educational concepts necessary for the development of our students. Students who learn usually do so in spite of rather than because of adequate instruction.

If cultural diversity is a constructive concept and not just another catch phrase, the educational process that produces our future generations must include maximum opportunities for creative approaches to learning the arts as well as the sciences. Teachers must begin by recognizing and respecting the differences in student learning styles. How a student processes information is directly related to his/her academic success. Administrators must be willing to redirect available resources to support

ELLIS MARSALIS

these creative approaches with the same enthusiasm that traditional approaches receive. Then and only then can cultural diversity become a reality in our educational system.

CHORUS #1

MARSALIS: We were talking about what has happened to the high schools. The high school has become a way station to a university with little else of any significance. These schools spend too much time focusing on whether or not people have a high enough SAT score to get into college. And where I'm from, there may be only about four or five of those schools that really present themselves as college preps. Some of the other schools, inner-city schools, have a lot of problems. They need a certain kind of leadership—there's sometimes very little community support. There's a lot of hooliganism going on, and they don't necessarily identify any track at all, so you find few schools in the inner city that say, "We are college prep." You see?

McCLUSKEY: Let's say that you need a transition in some places. I guess in most places it's that point where young students go into middle school and high school. Here middle school goes up to eighth grade and high school starts in ninth grade. Between, say, grades eight and ten, you begin to see people dropping out.

MARSALIS: Yeah, that's junior high. Middle school now includes fourth, fifth, and sixth grade. Junior high is seventh, eighth, and ninth. And high school is tenth, eleventh, and twelfth. Some high schools start in the eighth grade, but basically that's how it breaks down.

Singular Voice, Several Sounds

McCLUSKEY: Let's say that you had the money and a model school, and you were catching the brothers coming through, since we're trying to funnel some of this toward African American males. Say you saw them coming through the eighth grade—do you have any sense of art education or curriculum change or just deportment or . . .

MARSALIS: First of all, most of the changes I'd make wouldn't cost a dime.

McCLUSKEY: Is that right?

MARSALIS: Eighth grade is too late. Let's look at two kinds of students. One kind of student can go into a school situation that is structured to a point where that student can function, can learn and progress. The other kind of student has need for a special kind of attention, and cannot be expected to come in and function and learn routinely. For example, some people have attention deficit disorder. Others, because of the foods that they eat or their parents ate, are wired. They eat a lot of sugar. And then there are some that have medical or mental problems, period. Obviously, this needs to be addressed on another level. But as long as we have teachers on the payroll and we have students, we really need to have a total elimination of first grade, second, third, fourth, fifth. It causes a division in the thinking of the teachers. You find teachers who say, "I teach sixth grade." Hey, what is that? Either you're a teacher or you're not.

McCLUSKEY: It's funny that you said that. Just today I was sitting next to a woman who was saying that she teaches third grade—she doesn't teach sixth grade, she wants to teach only third grade. I said to myself pretty much what you've just said: "If you're a teacher, you're a teacher."

122

MARSALIS: I can understand anybody who says, "The age of children I like to teach is this age." But here's the key: standardized tests are already being used in the school. I don't know if they go down to first grade or not. When a kid obviously has a deficiency, the old-school thinking was that if you put him in a class where kids are strong, that will help to motivate him. We know that is a joke. All it does is reinforce the feelings of inferiority. If you have a class of thirty people, and twenty of them have a deficiency in English and ten of them don't, you assign those twenty kids to a teacher who specializes in remedial work. Forget first grade. The other ten go to a different teacher because they are prepared to move ahead. You do the same thing with math and with all the other subjects, and you begin to utilize teachers in ways that benefit the students.

For example, a curse of the education system is the tenure track. That's a can of worms. There are also systems that have actually started to give year-by-year contracts. Of course, a lot of that has to do with fiscal realities more so than philosophical. Nonetheless, I think that if you give certain kinds of people the opportunity to slide by, they will do so. So if a teacher is sliding by and really has not kept up—perhaps he was certified at a school with some C's and got on in—instead of trying to make an English teacher out of him, you make him into a glorified monitor. You don't call him that, of course. But what you do is have him work with those students who could best learn by simply copying out of a book. That is a method of learning that is considered primitive by the Harvard crowd that makes decisions for the city schools. Some kids just can't sit there and read and conceptualize, so you have them sit down and open up their textbook, and just copy out of it. First they are working on penmanship; second, you are reinforcing spelling; and third, writing something

123

down affects the cognitive process—just the act of writing it down. So you give these people who are really not that strong in teaching skills the job of seeing that the student copies that book. From the grading standpoint, if you've got fifteen pages to copy and you copy all fifteen pages, you get one grade; you copy ten, you get another grade. So it's not difficult to grade, and you've made use of some deadwood that you cannot fire. If you try to fire these teachers, you'll have lawsuits on your hands. So put them to use in ways that are more constructive, and they'll want to come to school cause they don't have to do nothing.

McCLUSKEY: Any way that music plays a role in this? Suppose you've got to get the same . . .

MARSALIS: No, I ain't got to no music yet.

McCLUSKEY: It's coming.

MARSALIS: I ain't got to no music and art yet because if you don't take care of the business over here [basic educational skills], there's no sense in even discussing music. It's sort of like discussing the icing and we have nobody to bake the cake.

RESPONSIBILITY

This speech was delivered at California State University– Northridge in 1993.

I congratulate each of you for maintaining the discipline and tenacity it takes to complete the process of graduating from a university. You have reached a milestone in your educational career. However, as you congratulate yourself for this significant achievement, it is also time to reflect on the responsibility that accompanies this achievement.

124

The *American Heritage Dictionary* defines *responsibility* as "involving personal accountability or ability to act without guidance or superior authority." It further states that one should be "capable of making moral or rational decisions on one's own and therefore answerable for one's behavior." It is this concept of responsibility I wish to share with you today.

As a youngster growing up in New Orleans and surrounded by music, I knew I loved it, but I was not made aware of the professional opportunities available. When I entered Dillard University as a freshman in 1951, New Orleans was a racially segregated city, and career opportunities in all areas were severely limited for African Americans. I had recently discovered the music of Charles Christopher Parker, Jr., a.k.a. the Bird, and John Burks Gillespie, a.k.a. "Dizzy," but, with the exception of one member, the music faculty at Dillard University was totally unsympathetic to the idea of music majors developing jazz skills. I found myself in the midst of a giant contradiction. I was a music major at a predominantly black university in New Orleans, Louisiana, the birthplace of jazz, where the music faculty was singing the praises of European concert music and condemning America's only indigenous musical contribution to world culture: *jazz*. I began to question faculty about this anti-jazz attitude and was greeted with rhetorical statements and terse rebuffs.

Being two months shy of my seventeenth birthday and short on both maturity and diplomacy, I did not endear myself to my superiors at the university. While I knew something was incorrect about their negative attitudes toward the music of my heroes, my youthful innocence and overly protective parents rendered me cautious to the point of timidity. Seeing no immediate solution to the problem, I began to view the university as a place I went to in the day and the club as a refuge at night.

I was constantly bombarded with advice regarding the performance of music professionally by people who were neither performers nor patrons of my beloved jazz music. My parents said that music was too risky and suggested I get a degree in business so I would have something to fall back on. The music faculty suggested music education so I would be able to teach and have something to fall back on. A friend of my father said I should major in math because I could get a job with a math degree. He then asked what did I want to do and I replied, "I want to be a musician." He replied, "You can't make a living being a musician." When I gave the example of Capitol recording artist Nat "King" Cole as being a successful musician, he retorted, "There's only one of him," to which I replied there was only one of *me*. He did not bother to reply.

I managed to graduate four years later, and while some of my friends graduated cum laude, I was pleased to finish "thank you, lordy." After graduation I immediately made two promises to myself: (1) I would go to New York and play with the giants of the jazz world, and (2) I would never become a teacher. Needless to say, I didn't keep either promise.

As I share these examples with you, I am mindful of the fact that many, if not all, of you have heard these same or similar comments from parents, relatives, friends, and a few well-meaning strangers. However, the decisions you make throughout your lifetime come with responsibilities to be met. When I decided that I wanted to be a jazz musician, I did so fully realizing there were no nightclubs in New Orleans willing to pay musicians to experiment. As a young neophyte, I was very critical of many local club owners who would not permit us to play long solos at extremely fast tempos while their customers wanted to dance and be entertained with the latest in popular music. My not being able to appreciate their point of view precipitated numerous arguments with club owners—none of which I won. As I got older and began to realize the futility of my position, it became increasingly evident that I was not exhibiting responsible behavior.

I was also very critical of other musicians who were not inclined to play the music I wanted to play and to practice long

ELLIS MARSALIS

hours for the intangible reward of personal satisfaction. My intolerance was but one more example of irresponsible behavior. I felt that a total commitment to the development of my craft was the only responsibility to be met. My very brief tenure as a nightclub owner helped me to understand responsibility on a different level.

My father allowed me to convert a house we owned into a nightclub. The venture lasted approximately six months. I found it to be virtually impossible to meet the responsibilities of both club owner and serious musician. Checking inventories, meeting tax deadlines, payroll, licenses, and personnel changes were only a few of the responsibilities I was not prepared to accept. I felt more responsible to developing myself as a jazz player than as a nightclub owner.

By this time I was married and was confronted with even larger responsibilities. As a young aspiring jazz musician, I had created a fantasy world in which I would learn to play, work with the world's great jazzmen, and live happily ever after. As a married adult, I found that the fantasy had become a pipe dream.

If you wish to assess your current position, here are two questions you may wish to ask yourself: What do I really want to do? If I continue doing what I am doing the way I am doing it, will I achieve it? Becoming a responsible person is a lifelong challenge. We are told that we must achieve success without being told that success is a journey, not a destination. That journey begins with one's acceptance of countless responsibilities. These two questions will assist you in evaluating your life while helping you to focus. As you reflect on your academic experience here, try to recall as much as you can about the learning process.

What role did your professors play in your learning process? Were your professors really here to "educate" you, or is this something you alone can do? What is your responsibility in this educational process? Did you pursue a degree so you might have something to "fall back on," or were you seeking a quality education?

In some ways a university is like a supermarket. There are lots of items from which to choose, but you cannot take them all. It is your responsibility to investigate what is available and make your decisions carefully but wisely. Did you approach your education in this manner?

The current picture for university graduates in the job market is not always cheerful. However, we live in a world of global economic opportunities, and when someone says you are going to have a problem finding a job, remember this: Every situation that is viewed as a problem is merely an opportunity in disguise.

If you are in the right place at the right time with the right equipment and the right attitude, you will without a doubt be responsible.

CHORUS #2

McCLUSKEY: I have read that when you were growing up, it was possible for a young brother to learn how to play in many ways. There were what I'm going to call apprenticeships to the black marching bands, or you could hang out in clubs or learn it in other ways. In other words, it sounds like the resources that we were talking about bringing to the school system were at one time much more available outside of school. From what you were saying, somehow kids were motivated to want to be musicians or to go out and find who these people were or find the outlet.

MARSALIS: Well, first of all, we're talking about New Orleans when you're talking about me, which is by no means the same as everybody else's town. We're also

ELLIS MARSALIS

talking about music that was more communal. The evolution of jazz from simplicity to complexity got a big boost from Louis Armstrong. There were people before him, but he was the first great jazz musician and improviser. He played a lot of blues, he played songs with very simple form, and he played for dances, picnics, weddings, whatever. It was a communal music and it was a communal experience, and the music was simple to grasp. Now move ahead some sixty years, past two world wars and two so-called police actions with Korea and Vietnam, and you get people like Charlie Parker and Thelonious Monk and John Coltrane, whose music is extremely complex. You also move away from community, in terms of the community that nurtured a Louis Armstrong. Our community exploded at least by 1964. That was an amazing year to me because two things occurred, which really didn't have anything to do with each other, but they both had an effect on American culture. One, that was the year the Beatles came to America, and two, it was the year that the Civil Rights Bill was passed.

McCLUSKEY: Also Schwerner, Goodman, and Chaney.

MARSALIS: Yeah, right, Schwerner, Goodman, and Chaney, also. All this was a continuation of what a lot of other people had started and done. I mean that in and of itself it was not as unique as either of those two events. Man, the white population has never been the same since the Beatles came to this country. Elvis didn't do for them what the Beatles did. The Beatles were a phenomenon, as was what ultimately occurred with the passage of the Civil Rights Bill. Those two don't have anything specifically to do with each other, but they were two phenomenal events. The complexity of jazz music reached a pinnacle in the 1960s. We could say it reached the zenith in 1967 because that's the year that John Coltrane died. John Coltrane in his music was really the last significant innovator at the level of Charlie Parker.

McCLUSKEY: *Love Supreme* or beyond even *Love Supreme*?

MARSALIS: Well, just him. There is a composite body of work that represents John Coltrane's contribution. I want to try to evaluate which is better than what. There is a progression he made from sideman to leader and from 1960, when he made *My Favorite Things*, which was a pretty big recording for him. What he was doing with that was a manifestation of an academic approach to our music, another stage of it, and that was basically the pinnacle of the whole thing. After that things started to decline, because in 1970 Miles made *Bitches' Brew*, which essentially was fusion. It wasn't nearly as challenging as the stuff that Miles's group had done with Wayne and Herbie in the sixties. I think what we start to get by 1970 is another beginning, and in the beginning of anything the simplistic aspect is most prominent.

McCLUSKEY: I'm curious about the image of the musician presented to the public, an image like that in the "Bird" story, where he came out of the stands as Charlie Nobody, Charlie from Kansas City, and the next thing you know he's Bird. The film left out the whole process of how he moved from one to the other. Of course he was practicing, right? He was somewhere practicing hard. So what the media emphasize is the self-destructive behavior of the musician, as if he is almost fated to go that way. At least, that's how it

ELLIS MARSALIS

appears in the earlier versions. How are musicians of your generation and younger dealing with the baggage of that whole image, and do you sense a different mission as an artist, a musician, than before?

MARSALIS: Yes.

McCLUSKEY: Where is that coming from? Is that coming from looking at the past and learning from their mistakes?

MARSALIS: No. I think in some cases it's a different breed of dog. First of all, jazz has become a lot more mainstream. In earlier years the jazz musicians were part of a subculture that played in nightclubs where people went to have fun and pick up women. I remember a friend of mine telling me about how Billie Holliday used to sing at Pa's and Jerry's, the joint where the white guys used to go to meet black women in New York City. That whole environment took on different proportions. It's not that we didn't have drug addicts and drunkards and all the rest of that, it's that all of a sudden there was an opportunity for the jazz musician to function beyond the limitations of clubs that were run by gangsters. And now you have people like Joshua Redman, who is the son of Dewey, who went to Harvard. And you have the kinds of things that my kids do, and more and more young musicians who don't function and don't get on bad habits. And it's not really just a black thing. Cause believe me, man, we [*laughs*] were not alone. I think a lot of it was a sign of the times.

McCLUSKEY: In terms of a healthier outlook and a more serious appreciation?

MARSALIS: Yeah, it's in the ether. Now you go into

regular grocery stores and there are sections of health food. There's a growth that's taking place.

McCLUSKEY: Particularly with the artists? I guess what we have to worry about at some point is the audience.

MARSALIS: The audience is even better. I mean, I would imagine there was a time when it would have been virtually impossible for me to come to a place like this to play the music that we're playing. I don't really see anything like that actually happening at all.

McCLUSKEY: I'm glad to see the musicians lasting longer and working in larger contexts, but I'm a little distressed that not enough of the music is being heard by the younger folk. It isn't on the radio enough.

MARSALIS: But it was never on the radio. It's more on the radio now than it's ever been. Those NPR stations, there's a lot of them, and at some point in time they'll play some jazz. They're community stations.

McCLUSKEY: It's the younger listeners I'm thinking about.

MARSALIS: A reporter came to a meeting and asked me about students with music education. And I said, "Man, I think American students need to be educated, period. Not just in music. I think there's a gross miseducation occurring, and it's across the board. And I don't think it makes sense to separate music and stick it over there. I think that it's possible to do these great things over there, and this thing over here is either going to take care of itself or there is no problem with it." That's one of the main things that I think we need to be addressing. A great article in the *Atlantic Monthly* quoted a man as saying that the system is dead but they won't bury the corpse. I think that we have a charge to really educate America. My son Wynton said that the

ELLIS MARSALIS

next level of consciousness is not going to be about race. I said that may be true, but ain't nobody going to reach it unless they embrace the realities of where they are and how they got where they are, and if that means you deal with race, then you've got to deal with race.

A JAZZ MUSICIAN'S WORK ETHIC

Becoming a jazz musician requires the same dedication to ideals and principles that is emphasized in the other, more traditional areas of study (medicine, law, business, etc.). However, that message is all too often lost in the imagery popularized by the electronic and print media. Television, newspapers, trade magazines, and supermarket scandal sheets consistently elevate mediocre performances with high levels of praise, where a lower level of amusement is obviously the objective of many of the recipients. As a practicing jazz musician, I feel it incumbent upon me to share some personal thoughts about the work ethic and the development of a professional philosophy.

Be patient. Seek to discover your assets and utilize them. Also, honestly recognize your liabilities so you can work toward their early demise. *Practice* not for showmanship but for a clear delivery of the message only honest music presents. The object of showmanship is to be seen. This practice diverts the audience's attention away from the weak skills of one who is ill prepared. If you cannot present your music without the ostentatious display of theatrics, you should re-evaluate your goals.

In order to speak with clarity through your instrument, you must visit each note personally. While some notes may have more weight than others, they are all important in the total presentation of your performance. If you are going to take the time to develop the skill of jazz improvisation, plan to use those skills courageously and honestly. Develop the courage to create along with the skill to perform.

Develop productive listening skills. If listening is to be productive, your choice of music must transcend the mediocrity of

_____ 133

popular entertainment that permeates the electronic media. If jazz is going to be the medium of expression for your creative endeavors, take the necessary time to research performances recorded by the jazz masters, especially on your instrument.

Do not allow the trade publications to define the medium for you. While these publications perform a necessary function in the total scheme of the music business, they seldom consider aesthetic criticism as their raison d'être. Their survival depends largely upon amassing a readership that supports their advertisers.

The jazz performer must strive to stretch him/herself. Each performance should reflect a change for the better, especially in rehearsals. Ensemble rehearsals and private practice sessions are critical to the individual growth of the developing student. This is where most of the individual progress will occur, not in public performances. Public performances contribute to personal development only when finely honed skills are on display.

Each performance should be a time to:

•Share what you have learned with an audience. Help the audience to experience the quality that comes from an honest performance.

•Evaluate your performance so you will know what to practice for self-improvement.

•Purge yourself of the incessant temptation toward mediocrity. Very often we play a part or a solo just well enough to get by. An enthusiastic performance usually produces an enthusiastic response, just as an honest performance will produce an honest response.

•Dress in a manner befitting the performance. Your work attire sends a message to the audience reflecting your attitude toward your presentation. The effectiveness of your performance is both visual and aural.

•Avoid mind-altering stimulants unless they are medically prescribed. A sober mind produces a sober performance.

•Practice punctuality. Being on time also reflects your attitude about your performance. If it is worth performing, it is worth starting on time.

•Remember this principle: Be in the *right place* at the *right time* with the *right attitude* and the *right equipment* ready to do the job.

Overtime

7. Four Poems

SLAM, DUNK, & HOOK

Fast breaks. Lay ups. With Mercury's
Insignia on our sneakers,
We outmaneuvered the footwork
Of bad angels. Nothing but a hot
Swish of strings like silk
Ten feet out. In the roundhouse
Labyrinth our bodies
Created, we could almost
Last forever, poised in midair
Like storybook sea monsters.
A high note hung there
A long second. Off
The rim. We'd corkscrew
Up & dunk balls that exploded
The skullcap of hope & good
Intention. Bug-eyed, lanky,
All hands & feet . . . sprung rhythm.
We were metaphysical when girls
Cheered on the sidelines.
Tangled up in a falling,
Muscles were a bright motor
Double-flashing to the metal hoop

Nailed to our oak.
When Sonny Boy's mama died
He played nonstop all day, so hard
Our backboard splintered.
Glistening with sweat, we jibed
& rolled the ball off our
Fingertips. Trouble
Was there slapping a blackjack
Against an open palm.
Dribble, drive to the inside, feint,
& glide like a sparrow hawk.
Lay ups. Fast breaks.
We had moves we didn't know
We had. Our bodies spun
On swivels of bone & faith,
Through a lyric slipknot
Of joy, & we knew we were
Beautiful & dangerous.

SONGS FOR MY FATHER

I told my brothers I heard
You & mother making love,
Your low moans like a blues
Bringing them into the world.
I didn't know if you were laughing
Or crying. I held each one down
& whispered your song in their ears.
Sometimes I think they're still jealous
Of our closeness, having forgotten
We had to square-off & face each other,
My fists balled & cocked by haymakers.
That spring I lifted as many crossties

YUSEF KOMUNYAKAA

As you. They can't believe I can
Remember when you had a boy's voice.

*

You were a quiet man
Who'd laugh like a hyena
On a hill, with your head
Thrown back, gazing up at the sky.
But most times you just worked
Hard, rooted in the day's anger
Till you'd explode. We always
Walked circles around
You, wider each year,
Hungering for stories
To save us from ourselves.
Like a wife who isn't touched,
We had to do something bad
Before you'd look into our eyes.

*

We spent the night before Easter
Coloring eggs & piling them into pyramids
In two crystal punch bowls.
Our suits, ties, white shirts, shoes,
All lined up for the next day.
We had memorized our passages
From the bible, about the tomb
& the angel rolling back the stone.
You were up before daybreak,
In the sagebrush, out among goldenrod
& mustard weed, hiding the eggs
In gopher holes & underneath roots.
Mother always argued with you,
Wondering why you made everything so hard.

*

Four Poems

We stood on a wooden platform
Facing each other with sledgehammers,
A copper-tipped sieve sunken into the ground
Like a spear, as we threaded on five foot
Of galvanized pipe for the pump.
As if tuned to some internal drum,
We hammered the block of oak
Placed on top of the pipe.
It began inching downward
As we traded blows—one for you,
One for me. After a half hour
We threaded on another five foot. The sweat
Gleamed on our shirtless bodies, father
& son tied to each other till we hit water.

*

Goddamn you. Goddamn you.
If you hit her again, I'll sail through
That house like a dustdevil.
Everyone & everything here
Is turning against you,
That's why I had to tie the dog
To a tree before you could chastise us.
He darted like lightning through the screen door.
I know you'll try to kill me
When it happens. You know
I'm your son & it's bound to happen.
Sometimes I close my eyes till I am
On a sea of falling dogwood blossoms,
But someday this won't work.

*

I confess. I am the ringleader
Who sneaked planks out of the toolshed,

YUSEF KOMUNYAKAA

Sawed & hammered together the wagon.
But I wasn't fool enough to believe
That you would've loved our work.
So, my brothers & I dug a grave
In the corner of the field for our wagon
That ran smooth as a Nat King Cole
Love ballad. We'd pull it around
The edge of our world & rebury it
Before the 5 o'clock mill whistle blew.
I bet it's still there, the wood gray
& light as the ribs of my dog Red
After somebody gunned him down one night.

*

You banged a crooked nail
Into a pine slab,
Wanting me to believe
I shouldn't have been born
With hands & feet
If I didn't do
Your kind of work.
You hated my books.
Sometimes at dusk,
I faced you like that
Childhood friend you trained
Your heart to always run
Against, the horizon crimson
As the eyes of a fighting cock.

*

I never asked how you
Passed the driver's test,
Since you could only write
& read your name. But hell,

You were good with numbers;
Always counting your loot.
That Chevy truck swerved
Along back roads night & day.
I watched you use wire
& sunlight to train
The strongest limbs,
How your tongue never obeyed
The foreman, how the truck motor
Was stunted, frozen at sixty.

*

You wanted to fight
When I told you that a woman
Can get rid of a man
With a flake of lye
In his bread each day.
When you told her what I said
I bet the two of you made love
Till the thought flew out of your head.
Now, when you stand wax-faced
At the door, your eyes begging
Questions as you mouth wordless
Songs like a red-belly perch,
Assaying the scene for what it is,
I doubt if love can part my lips.

*

Sometimes you could be
That man on a red bicycle,
With me on the handlebars,
Just rolling along a country road
On the edge of July, honeysuckle
Lit with mosquito hawks.

YUSEF KOMUNYAKAA

We rode from under the shady
Overhang, back into sunlight.
The day bounced off car hoods
As the heat & stinking exhaust
Brushed against us like a dragon's
Roar, nudging the bike with a tremor,
But you steered us through the flowering
Dogwood like a thread of blood.

*

You lean on a yard rake
As dry leaves & grass smolder
In a ditch in mid March,
Two weeks before your sixty-first
Birthday. You say I look happy,
I must be in love. It is 1986,
Five months before your death.
You toss a stone at the two dogs
Hooked together in a corner of the yard.
You smile, look into my eyes
& say you want me to write you a poem.
I stammer for words. You
Toss another stone at the dogs
& resume raking the leafless grass.

*

I never said thanks for Butch,
The wooden dog you pulled by a string.
It was ugly as a baldheaded doll.
Patched with wire & carpenter's glue, something
I didn't believe you had ever loved.
I am sorry for breaking it in half.
I never meant to make you go
Stand under the falling snowflakes

With your head bowed on Christmas
Day. I couldn't look at Butch
& see that your grandmother Julia,
The old slave woman who beat you
As if that's all she knew, had put love
Into it when she carved the dog from oak.

*

I am unlike Kikuji
In Kawabata's *Thousand Cranes,*
Since I sought out one of your lovers
Before you were dead.
Though years had passed
& you were with someone else,
She thought I reminded her
Of a man she'd once known.
She pocketed the three dollars.
A big red lampshade bloodied
The room, as if held by a mad
Diogenes. Yes, she cried out,
But she didn't sing your name
When I planted myself in her.

*

You spoke with your eyes
Last time I saw you, cramped
Between a new wife & the wall. You couldn't
Recognize funeral dirt stamped down
With dancesteps. Your name & features half
X-ed out. I could see your sex,
Your shame, a gold-toothed pout,
As you made plans for the next house you'd build,
Determined to prove me wrong. I never knew
We looked so much like each other. Before

YUSEF KOMUNYAKAA

I could say I loved you, you began talking money,
Teasing your will with a cure in Mexico.
You were skinny, bony, but strong enough to try
Swaggering through that celestial door.

TO HAVE DANCED WITH DEATH

The black sergeant first class
who stalled us on the ramp
didn't kiss the ground either.

When two hearses sheened up to the plane
& government silver-gray coffins
rolled out on silent chrome coasters,

did he feel better? The empty left leg
of his trousers shivered as another hearse
with shiny hubcaps inched from behind a building . . .

his three rows of ribbons rainbowed
over the forest of faces through
plate glass. Afternoon sunlight

made surgical knives out of chrome
& brass. He half smiled when
the double doors opened for him

like a wordless mouth taking back promises.
The room of blue eyes averted his.
He stood there, searching

his pockets for something:
maybe a woman's name & number
worn thin as a Chinese fortune.

I wanted him to walk ahead,

to disappear through glass,
to be consumed by music

that might move him like Sandman Sims,
but he merely rocked on his good leg
like a bleak & soundless bell.

COPACETIC MINGUS

> "'Mingus One, Two and Three.
> Which is the image you want the world to see?'"
> —Charles Mingus, *Beneath the Underdog*

Heartstring. Blessed wood
& every moment the thing's made of:
ball of fatback
licked by fingers of fire.
Hard love, it's hard love.
Running big hands down
the upright's wide hips,
rocking his moon-eyed mistress
with gold in her teeth.
Art & life bleed
into each other
as he works the bow.
But tonight we're both a long ways
from the Mile High City,
1973. Here in New Orleans
years below sea level,
I listen to *Pithecanthropus
Erectus:* Up & down, under
& over, every which way—
thump, thump, dada—ah, yes.

YUSEF KOMUNYAKAA

Wood heavy with tenderness,
Mingus fingers the loom
gone on Segovia,
dogging the raw strings
unwaxed with rosin.
Hyperbolic bass line. Oh, no!
Hard love, it's hard love.

Four Poems

To the Defense

8. The Real Deal

Brothers often tell me that the problem with a lot of our young black men is that they lack common respect and motivation, or they just don't understand that listening to rap music every day is one reason why they aren't learning anything. The sad part of this is that the brothers who say these things work as mentors to the young men that these statements reflect upon. I am often asked what is wrong with these "young little niggas." My reply the first time was, "Did you ever *ask* these young men what they really needed? And why would you ever call another brother a 'nigger'?" I want to tell a lot of you, my brothers, that most of us don't even deal with our own personal pain, our own personal suffering, or even with what our own personal definition of manhood is. The sad truth is that a number of us lack self-esteem and self-confidence, and because of this, too many of us use the little head between our legs as a measurement of our manhood. Not enough of us realize that manhood is the harmony of mind and spirit and not the size of or frequency with which one uses his penis.

NOT ALL BROTHERS ARE GOOD ROLE MODELS FOR YOUNGER BROTHERS

The sad reality is that just because a man's skin is black and just because he has a job and goes to church every Sunday, that does not make him an ideal role model for most of our young black men on the streets today. I spoke at a few churches this year, and I was amazed to see how many men lacked faith in the God that I know watches over me. I remember relating some of my experiences on the street to the story of Jesus in the wilderness, and how Satan tried to tempt Jesus into turning water into wine to make his stay in the desert more enjoyable and stones into bread to curb his hunger. I continued my presentation, and then I paused and asked the men in these congregations, "How many of you have faith?" Every man in the church raised his hand, and there were scattered chants of "well," "amen," "preach, brother," and even a few "ummmm ummm, got to have that faith." I then went on to ask my brothers, "Why aren't you all out there in the wilderness?" I explained that the wilderness is not in here (inside the church), the wilderness is out there (the streets, the world). We can no longer continue to preach to the saved and forget those who need to know that somebody somewhere cares for them. I then reassured my brothers that I was not questioning the level of their faith, but I wanted to let them know that, like mine, it has to move to the next level.

Earlier this week I had an opportunity to listen to a man describe how successful he was, how his hard work had finally paid off, and how many important people he knew. He told me that he could go anywhere in the world because his cash flow was fat, that women see him as irresistible and a prize catch. He attends almost all of the who's who ("the lucky circuit") functions in Boston. When I finally had a second to say something, I asked him what he thought about our young black men. He quickly explained that "your people" (mine only), "those little niggas," don't know the first thing about work; that they are some "lazy piece o' shit beggars" trying to decrease his wallet; and that "all them little punks want to do is get their dicks wet— most of them are baby-making motherfuckas anyway; the whole damn bunch of them are lost" (I wonder why). He went on, "I ain't got the time for their bullshit, and hey, if they don't listen,

MICHAEL O'NEAL

I can't help them." His car phone rang, and he said that it was nice talking to me, and that I should contact him because he wants to help my organization as a volunteer. He eased off down the road in his BMW 635 csi.

This man is one reason why I say that not all brothers are good role models for our young black men. I truly thought about "pimp slapping" the home boy, but I can almost guarantee you that someone else will deliver that wake-up call to homey! From all of us. Until I met this brother, I always thought that a conversation took place between at least two people. I wanted to set him straight, but I hardly had a chance to speak. I could not see this brother as a mentor for a young man in our or any other organization. He does not listen. My brother talked *to* me and not *with* me, and many of our younger brothers need someone to listen to what they are feeling. In a worst-case scenario, a young man might need someone to listen to him because somebody dissed him and he wanted to shoot that brother. Or perhaps he slapped his girlfriend and he needs some guidance in how to control his anger. If my man had spoken to this brother, the outcome would have been almost predictable.

I almost always start my formal presentations with this statement about listening: "I think the greatest skill that a man can have is the ability to listen, because through listening all learning occurs." We must start listening and communicating to our young men that we love them and will support them, and that we have the ability to listen and be open. We must show that we can be compassionate toward them and nonjudgmental of the value system that the streets (and not always an adult) have taught them. Individually, we must also start to have the courage to listen to exactly how and why our young men don't respect us and why some of us "ain't" good role models. A lot of our younger brothers see some of us as "sellouts" and "house niggers," who are more than willing to front a brother to make sure that he doesn't live up to his fullest potential. They believe that such an adult has the resources to help but won't help unless he is needed for some statistical study to ensure the continuation of weak agencies.

THE REALITIES OF RAP AND HIP-HOP MUSIC, AND HOW OUR YOUNGER BROTHERS SEE US AND WHY THEY LACK RESPECT FOR US

YESTERDAY!!!!!

Most of us wonder why our young black men openly disrespect us, sometimes challenging our manhood to the point that a verbal and physical confrontation is imminent. Unfortunately, we never quite make the connection that we are responsible for why so many of our young brothers don't have the same understanding about their value system. Nevertheless, I wonder how many of you ever listened to Billie Holiday sing the "blues" or listened to John Coltrane's horn pierce your soul to help you cope with the twisted realities of being a black man facing the unyielding, spirit-crushing traditions that America perpetuates through racism. Because their music touched the core of how and what we were feeling, we somehow were better able to put our lives into perspective and maintain hope about our personal futures and the future of our people.

TODAY!!!!!

Today Billie Holiday has been replaced by Queen Latifah, MC Lyte, Yo Yo, Salt-N-Pepa, Sista Souljah, Bitches With Attitudes, Monie Love, and a host of other hot-chocolate rapping divas that bring the message of truth on the strength. My sisters are complemented by a warrior breed of brothers shaped out of the legacy of Malcolm X and Grand Master Flash. These brothers who have captured the attention of our young black men include Public Enemy, KRS-One, EPMD, Ice-T, Ice Cube, Eazy E, the Geto Boys, Scarface, 2 Live Crew, Eric B and

152

MICHAEL O'NEAL

Rakim, LL Cool J, Run-DMC, Shabba Ranks, the Jamaican Posse, Compton's Most Wanted, N.W.A., Heavy D & the Boyz, Big Daddy Kane, Das EFX, Ed O.G. and Da Bulldogs, and many more in the underground circuit.

These young women and men are singing the 1990s version of the blues, to a tune that reaches our children more effectively than the family, ministers, and current political leaders. Some of what adults fail to realize can be attributed to our own forgetting that in America and in many parts of the world, we as a race of men are considered "niggers," and our abilities are marginalized and relegated to an Amos 'n' Andy or Step'n Fetchit mode or to that of a gridiron superman. Rap and hip-hop have given our young men a platform from which to express their anger and frustrations—with themselves, America, you, me—their views about their sexuality and relationships with young women, the realities of death, God, faith, keeping their memory alive by making a baby, the need to make a child so that someone will love them back. The music expresses how the gang and drug cultures have shaped their community, their world. The music reflects the realities of the judicial system, prison, the police, and our failure as black men to listen and reach out to young men and validate their worth, their thinking mind. We must protect them and train them to be men. These themes are what the music speaks to, and the truth is what we have to deal with, and their anger and disdain for some of us. I know that the lyrics are offensive and explicit, and I don't refer to my sisters as "bitches" or "ho's" or to other black men as "niggers." The real truth of the matter is that no young black man came out of his mother's womb chanting, "The bitch better have my money" or "Suck my dick, bitch." We as men must realize that we have failed to set standards for our young men, and our failure to raise our young men firmly, compassionately, and with consistency and respect is a key reason why so many of them place so much value on protecting their already fragile egos. As one young man put it, "I'll annihilate any motherfucka that tries to dis me."

I have seen the streets over the past ten years become more like the setting for the film *Predator 2*. As another young man put it: "It's you or him; you got to flex and get your shit off first, and you better wreck the dude, too." This is the survival legacy (attitude) that we have allowed our young black men to embrace because of our nonparticipation in their development. They need coping mechanisms to handle potentially stressful and life-threatening situations. They need your input so that they can develop internal strength and restraint. I see far too many young black men take rides in what I call the "macho man cabs." One is a police car and the other is an ambulance. Most of the rides occur because some brother spent the afternoon ingesting liquid forty-ounce courage as a result of his frustration about not finding a job or about a failing relationship. With no way to constructively cope with his anger, his anxiety level rises to the point that the John Wayne Juice flowing through his veins has clouded his reasoning. He now decides to pull the trigger of his Mac 10 and send another brother to the doughnut underground only because he saw him laughing and speaking to his woman. The tragic and standard storyline: "He just started yelling. The next thing I saw was a gun, and my boyfriend pointing and firing it at my cousin Steven. Oh God, he's dead, he's dead. He thought he was trying to talk to me. My cousin is dead." This type of tragedy always makes the headlines—and another chapter of a promising young life has ended.

We must reclaim these young men as ours and be there to listen and teach them about the value of their life and the value of their brothers' life. I know that not all older brothers can bring this message to our young men or feel that they have something to offer. I would caution those older brothers who have an idea to preach to these young brothers, because in their reality what you say and how you say it can be hazardous to your health. Too many times a well-intentioned brother has approached a group of younger brothers, wanting to let them know that he is down to help them. The brother steps out of his

MICHAEL O'NEAL

450 SL and tries to rap about how hard work will pay off. To make a short story even shorter, these young brothers can smell a phony a mile away, so any message you decide to form your lips to speak better be on the strength. Otherwise you might find yourself getting your ass kicked or "ganked" for your gear. This is not to scare you but to let you know that these young brothers are tired of being tired and tired of hearing tired. Most of our young people feel that many in the older generation have accepted the belief that we have to reject and neglect our own culture and accept America's definition of how black people should be socialized into being that politically correct and by-the-book kind of guy.

Our young black men have seen us become toothless and declawed lions, and in some cases spineless braggarts, who cling to back-in-the-day stories of manly conquests that validate what we used to be in order to show them that we also understand today's world and their experiences. We are also viewed as complainers and as not being strong enough to stand up and fight for ourselves or them. Most of our young black men say, "Fuck that Martin Luther King 1960s turning-the-other-cheek bullshit. I ain't going out like a sucka. I'm taking motherfuckas out, I'm going out like a trooper."

My brothers, there is a new breed of young brother out there, and we need to be a part of their experience. We must help our young men understand the difference between negotiating and negrotiating.

THE BASTARDIZATION OF A GENERATION: WE MUST EMBRACE THESE YOUNG BLACK MEN AND "TEACH THEM HOW TO FISH, NOT GIVE THEM A FISH"

THE RESPONSIBILITY IN MALE RESPONSIBILITY

We have an opportunity and an obligation to raise our young black men. If we don't take the time to set realistic examples for them, we will continue to bastardize their generation. Most older men these days just shake their heads and toss their hands up in the air in disbelief and say, "Back in the day when I was coming up, I would have gotten my black ass whipped for acting and talking like these young boys do today." The fact is that "back in the day" is today; largely because we have not helped these young men to realize that certain behaviors will not be tolerated, we have only ourselves to blame for the disrespect that is openly practiced in our communities. The fact that a young black man of twelve or younger feels that he has the right to approach a women in her twenties or thirties and ask her to have sexual intercourse with him shows a profound disrespect. If you don't correct him, you unconsciously validate his belief system in allowing him to think that it's okay for him to speak to a woman in this disrespectful manner. If you don't jump off in his stuff and correct him, if you laugh and slap five with your boys, don't blame him when he disrespects your mother, your sister, your cousin or companion. You had an opportunity to set him straight and didn't. Blame yourself, homey.

The responsibility of older black men toward younger black men is to provide them with guidance and with an understanding that their *attitude* will affect their *altitude*. Among our other responsibilities is explaining the traditions that we embrace, and explaining why some of our black leaders have allowed the media to carefully orchestrate negative images of young black men as "gang bangers and drug dealers." Our role is to set the record straight and explain to our young men that they should not be afraid of being successful, that racism in America should not define their potential, that they are the most valuable resource that we have going, and that we will support them and have their backs.

When older black men suit up for the fight and reach out to their younger brothers, then and only then will attitudes change. However, we don't explain to them that excuses build bridges to nowhere and that as men we must have the courage and integ-

MICHAEL O'NEAL

rity to face adversity even when the cards are stacked against us. Then and only then will we have a true sense of what your character is and how well you as a man handle adversity.

A FATHER'S FIRST RESPONSIBILITY IS TO PROTECT HIS CHILD AND FAMILY

In June 1994 I spoke to a group of inmates at two major correctional institutions here in Boston. I asked them what they thought a father's first responsibility to his children is. Their responses were:
•to love them
•to provide them with a nice home
•to give them food
•to take them to the doctor's office when they are ill
•to spend time with them
•to educate them
I told the men that all of their responses were correct, but there was one response I had not heard that was critically important. I gave these brothers the following scenario: "I live in your neighborhood and my name is Jeffrey Dahmer. My favorite people in history were Adolf Hitler, Mussolini, Son of Sam, and Jack the Ripper. I'm a rapist and a pedophile. I've noticed your beautiful sons, and I know that I can have them any time I want. You, the father, are locked up and won't be out any time soon." The faces of the brothers became twisted, and they started to grind their teeth and clench their fists. I again asked these brothers what is a father's first responsibility to his family. Brothers then started giving me my personal number one answer: "To protect them." I then asked these brothers, "How in the hell can you protect your family if you are in here?" The room went dead quiet, and I broke the silence by saying, "If you can't stay out of prison for yourself, then stay out for your children's sake." The brothers started murmuring amongst themselves and agreed that they have to change their lifestyle

when they get back out on the set (the streets) so that they can protect their families.

I gave these brothers a few more scenarios to illustrate how important a role they play in their children's lives and why they have to be there for their children.

Scenario #1

Your lady and you have a beautiful baby girl. Your little girl turned three years old today, and she loves you to the point that she follows you everywhere you go until you pick her up and tenderly kiss her little hands. However, as time goes on, your employer promotes you to a more responsible position; one day your little girl turns twelve years old, and she notices that you are always too busy for her. Lately you haven't been the most affectionate person in the world. Now she is sixteen, and you reject her desire to have her daddy physically cuddle her like he did when she was a little girl, making her feel safe and loved.

She walks out of the house, her eyes filled with tears. She walks for ten or twelve blocks, ignoring the heckling and jeers directed at her well-developed body. She fails to hear them because you have avoided her and her questions about why she is changing and why you have changed. She feels that you no longer love her, and she feels that she has angered you or disappointed you. Now she feels very ugly and unwanted. She quickens her pace and tries to hide the tears that are streaming profusely down her cheeks. As she walks, her toe catches the lip of the curb, and she stumbles and bumps into a man. She quickly apologizes to him for being so clumsy; he tells her that it isn't every day that he is bumped into by a beautiful angel. She enthusiastically says, "Really? You think I'm a beautiful angel?" The man looks her in the eyes, then tenderly kisses her hand (just like you used to) and tells her his name (let's call him Vance).

Three months go by, and you start to notice that your little girl is wearing some very revealing clothes. When you sharply ask her where she's going, she tells you "out" with a friend. You ask how old is this friend. She says he's seventeen and that they met at school (Vance is twenty-five). The phone rings and it's your boss. You try to stop her as she walks out the door, but your boss's tone demands your undivided attention. You watch her walk out to the street, where an older, well-dressed brother helps her into his black, chrome-trimmed BMW L7. You suddenly feel your heart sink. Your boss's voice becomes increasingly lost in the numbing realization that your angelic little girl is now in the company of the neighborhood gangster Mac. You start to say to yourself, "What have I done, and why was I too busy to listen and guide her away from that kind of man?" You must protect your child!

Scenario #2

Your son complains that there are some hoodie dudes at school dissing him by taking his money and gear (clothes) in front of people. He tells you at least once a day that he needs your help and advice to get them up off of him. You start questioning his manhood, telling him that no punk ever took your clothes or made a fool out of you, and you were always man enough to knock any motherfucker into next week with yesterday's clothes. Your son says to you, "But Dad, they have guns, and they don't fight up-and-up anymore. Their whole crew flexes on one dude." You angrily respond, "If you hadn't spent so much time on your mother's damn breast, you would be a man now and not some whimpering faggot getting his ass whipped every day. Boy, you got to be tough and stand up to these punks. Go upside their heads and let them know that you ain't the one." You tell him to stop acting like a bitch and be a man.

Your son leaves the house for school the next day feeling thoroughly dissed. He has to deal with the reality that those hoods threatened to kill him if he came back to school while they were on the set. However, all he remembers is what you said about being a man and not a punk. He walks across the school-yard angry and seeking to regain his manhood. He approaches the group of brothers who have terrorized him for the past eight months. He starts pointing his finger in the face of their leader. He walks closer and punches the leader in the face. The leader hits the ground and your son says, "Get up, punk." The other boy reaches inside his coat and pulls out a snub-nose 357. Later on that evening, you hear a knock at the door, and you think that it's your son coming in later than he is allowed. You quickly open the door and are surprised to see a police officer there. You ask the officer what's wrong, and he solemnly tells you that your son was shot and killed earlier today at school and that they tried to reach you at work. The cop asks you if your son would have any reason to attack the leader of a gang in front of ten gang members. You hit your knees weeping. "My son, my son, what have I done?"

My brothers, you must protect your children!!!!!

"NEGROTIATING"

I came up with this term a few years ago when I was speaking with a group of young black males at a local high school. I told them that while this word is very funny, its meaning could save your life on the street someday. I explained that the word "negrotiate" has distinct components, one being the *Negro ego,* and as I said before, these elements will get you a first-class ticket and in some cases a round-trip ride in one of the "macho man cabs."

The art of negrotiating is pretty straightforward. It includes how to deal with some of my brother's funky attitudes on the street and can even be implemented in the job environment, church, school, or anyplace you may encounter a person or group who are giving off a foul kind of "vibe." Such a vibe could potentially threaten your spiritual, mental, and physical well-being. A few scenarios will illustrate how to successfully negrotiate in your day-to-day life.

MICHAEL O'NEAL

Scenario #1

A brother approaches you on the street with a gun and asks you to kick over the valuables. Should you:

(A) Break into your Bruce Lee mode and take the gun from homey!
(B) Kick over the valuables.
(C) Tell homeboy to kiss your ass.
(D) Scream for help and make his shaking hand shake even more.

Scenario #2

A sister is your boss, and she tells you that you are in danger of losing your job if you come to work late once more. You know that she is in the process of a stressful divorce. Should you:

(A) Tell her that her being so picky is the reason why homeboy is jetting out of Dodge.
(B) Thank her for being gracious enough to give you another chance.
(C) Tell homegirl to kiss your (you know the rest).
(D) Tell everyone in the office she's a bitch with PMS and later remember that it's a family business.

Scenario #3

You're riding the train and a brother steps on your brand-new GrandMaMa sneakers. He tells you to watch where the fuck you're stepping. You notice he has three GrandMaMa-sized friends. Should you:

(A) Tell him to go fuck himself and learn how to see and walk.
(B) Say, "Excuse me, brother-my-bad, good lookout and I'll be more careful."
(C) Tell him that just because he's here with his punk-assed boys, that won't stop you from kicking his punk ass.
(D) Tell him, "Yo Mama."

The Real Deal

Scenario #4

You're at a party with your lady, and a brother disrespects her by calling her a bitch because she won't give him her attentions. Should you:

(A) Punch him out!
(B) Take your lady and leave the party.
(C) Defend her honor to the death.
(D) Run and hide.

Scenario #5

Your best friend tells you that you have extreme body odor. Should you:

(A) Smack him up.
(B) Thank him for being honest with you.
(C) End your friendship because of his saying this to you.
(D) Tell him it's his ass that's kicking.

Scenario #6

You have just met a sister who looks better than a batch of Miss Gurdey Maye's buttermilk biscuits. The two of you can't wait to have sex. She invites you into her apartment, and soon after you are in the mix. Suddenly she asks you to stop, because she's changed her mind. Should you:

(A) Slap her and tell her, "Not until I bust my nut, bitch."
(B) Honor her request and ask if she is all right.
(C) Laugh in her face and keep stroking.
(D) Ignore her request; you know she knows she wants it.

Scenario #7

You see your father sexually touching your five-year-old sister. Should you:

MICHAEL O'NEAL

(A) Ignore what you've seen.

(B) Tell your mother.

(C) Tell your sister never to tell anyone or something bad will happen to the family.

(D) Tell your sister it was her fault.

Scenario #8

You witness a drug dealer shoot a brother in the back of the head, killing him. The dealer knows that you saw him do it, and he says you will be next if you open your mouth. Should you:

(A) Kill him before he kills you, and risk a prison sentence.

(B) Talk to your parents and the police to let them know that this person will be after you if he thinks you've talked.

(C) Leave town as soon as possible.

(D) Forget you saw anything, and believe that this person won't harm you.

Scenario #9

You are stopped by the police and a cop says to you, "Nigger, what the fuck are you doing around here?" Should you:

(A) Say, "Going to visit your goddamn mammy."

(B) Ask, "Is there a reason for stopping me, sir?" and, if there is none, continue on your way. Ask for or look for a name and badge number.

(C) Say, "Fuck you, punk."

(D) Tell him that you are out trying to rob some white people.

Scenario #10

Your best friend dies of AIDS, and he leaves a note telling you that he is gay. The two of you hung tough. Your problem is that he's dead and people treat you like the two of you had it going on, and you're not gay. Should you:

(A) Pretend like you were not that close as friends.

(B) Speak up for your friend and let people think what they want.

(C) Destroy anything your friend ever gave you.

(D) Start having sex with as many women as possible to lose the gay image and save face.

If you chose response B in your answers to the ten life scenarios above, you have "negrotiated" successfully. However, if you chose any of the other answers, you will find that failing this test will cause you to kick ass, get your ass kicked, or even take a ride in one of the macho man cabs, a.k.a. the lifestyles of the raggedy and foolish cabs.

These are real-life scenarios, although some seem funny and tragic. The reality is that our young black men don't know how to deal in certain life situations; our young black men fall prey to their "Negro egos" because of their inability to reason, respond, or not respond to a heated and funky life situation that is guaranteed to land them in prison or the morgue, and because we refuse to listen and learn about their fears and needs. They feel that we are sellouts and Uncle Tom House Niggers who would rather lick master's boots than kick his ass. I truly don't want this image associated with my personal integrity or the integrity of my organization (Fathers, Inc.), but our not having time to spend with our younger brothers validates what they are saying about us. As painful as reality may be, we truly are shadows of the men our young black brothers see. We have become "all talk and no jock," and they desperately need to see some of us stand up and be counted. I would like those of you who will spend at least four hours in a nightclub this weekend to give at least one young brother fifteen minutes of your time. Don't be surprised if he thanks you for listening and caring about what he was feeling.

MICHAEL O'NEAL

MICHAEL'S TWO-STEP GUIDE TO HOW TO AVOID BECOMING A VICTIM OF YOUR NEGRO EGO

STEP 1: Each morning I hit my knees and thank God for letting me see another day.

STEP 2: After I finish saying my prayers, I leave my ego and pride on my bed and go out into the world. I let them fight each other all day and wear each other out. I am able to deal and work better for and with others because I left my ego and pride at home.

Bread, Fish, Fruit

9. What It Feels Like to Be a Problem

When I was asked to contribute to this collection of essays, I was told that it was to be called "The Problems of the Black Male in America." That the editors chose such a title, if only provisionally, and that I initially accepted it without question, is powerful testimony to the extent to which we had all accepted the notion that to be a black man in America in the 1990s is problematic.

All across the country, from Baltimore to Los Angeles, from Milwaukee to Atlanta, school officials are discussing the possibility of all-black, all-male schools as a solution to the problems of a generation. In May of 1991, the three-day meeting of the 21st Century Commission on African American Males was accompanied by pious pronouncements from educators, businessmen, and government officials about racism and the failures of society. While there was probably no cause and effect at work, a month later street vendors were selling t-shirts bearing the legend "Being a black man is the hardest job in America."

With all of this as evidence, it is tempting to take the bait, and to write about the already all too familiar (and if they *aren't*, they should be) laments about the problems that are part of being black and male. To do so, however, would be to accept complicity in the furthering of the primary black export to white America and the rest of the world: our pain, and ourselves as objects of entertainment.

The point is that while there are aspects of being a black man in modern-day America that are, to put it mildly, troublesome, the fact of my blackness does not mean that upon waking up each morning, I look in the mirror and exclaim, "Oh my God, I'm black!"

I do not want to minimize the struggles with the racism that continues to infect this country and that many of us still endure. And yet, whatever problems most black men face each day, at home, at work, or from society in general, we must—if we are honest—admit that things are better for most of us than they have ever been at any time in this country. Black men like me who are old enough to remember something of what life was like before the civil rights movement (even if we did not participate directly in it), and young enough to have taken advantage of and benefited from the opportunities the movement opened up, must admit how much our lives have changed in comparison to the lives of our fathers and grandfathers.

Given this, it seems to me that instead of crying the blues about how bad things are for black men, this generation must look at how—unforgivably when compared to the struggle, sacrifice, and courage of those who preceded us—it has failed by abdicating its leadership of the black community. Many black men have been content to pursue material success and ignore social concerns, have been eager to take advantage of black women disheartened by the dwindling numbers of eligible black men.

These last are the men who believe that, as a man I know once put it, "All you need to get over in D.C. is a Volvo and a bachelor's degree." Other members of their cohort are, on the surface, at least, political and "Afrocentric," the latest buzzword that translates to acceptability and political correctness. But listen to them talk for a while, and one soon discovers that they

DAVID NICHOLSON

have eschewed original thought for received wisdom. Few trouble themselves with reading the sources from which they draw their philosophy, if such a word can be applied to that random, chaotic, haphazard system of thought.

Instead, they parrot a party line that could be dismissed as mere arrogance were it not for the defensive note of compensation and self-pity. At its best, that party line is an understandable attempt at compensation in a world that each day proclaims that black men are lacking. At its worst it is a perversion of all that was noble about the civil rights movement, for it continues to celebrate the apotheosis of the "street nigger" that occurred in the late 1960s and 1970s, perpetuating a game devoted to the twin masturbatory satisfactions of blaming Whitey and preaching revolution.

For those black men, *white* men are to blame for the disgraceful increase in black teenage pregnancies. Never mind that nine months before these girls bore their babies, there were no white men prowling the streets of their neighborhoods seeking to despoil them. For them violent confrontation will solve black America's ills. Never mind that talk of revolution no longer scares white people, if indeed it ever did, and that the thing that really would—working to prepare young black men so that they could make up half the applicants to the freshmen classes at Harvard, Columbia, Yale, and Princeton, and be fully qualified for admission—is too hard to talk about.

The result is that Yeats's lines seem sadly applicable to the men I know, and the ones I don't know but whom I observe on the streets, on the subway, or talking to each other in restaurants or barbershops: The best of us lack all conviction. The worst are filled with passionate intensity.

It is true, of course, that black men have been victimized by centuries of white oppression and that in the 1970s and 1980s our victimization was abetted by a corps of self-indulgent, divisive feminists hell-bent on informing the world of the worst about their fathers, brothers, and husbands. But it seems to me

169

What It Feels Like to Be a Problem

that victims have only two choices: to acquiesce in the naming of themselves as victims and in their victimhood, or to take responsibility for their condition. Even in the period of our greatest trials in this country, no black man was a slave as the natural result of his inferiority to those who enslaved him. He may have lacked the power to prevent his bondage, but the historical record shows us, time and time again, black men preserving, against hardships inconceivable to most of us today, customs, heritage, family, dignity, and values.

The difference, I think, between this generation and those brave men who arrived in chains on these shores and managed not merely to endure but to prevail, is simply a matter of being willing to take responsibility for our lives. Today, too many black men are willing to excuse and to rationalize behavior that threatens all of us, black and white.

A hundred years ago I might have gone to bed at night with a shotgun in easy reach, sleeping fitfully and expecting to wake to the sound of hoofbeats or the voices of a gang of hooded whites. But though I am writing this in 1991, I confess to having breathed a sigh of relief when I turned thirty-five. Statistically, at least, my chances of dying violently at the hands of another black man had decreased significantly. I live aware that one day I may come home and find my house burglarized and my television, stereo, and computer destined to be sold out of the back of somebody's car or truck. The police that patrol my neighborhood have told people to stay out of the park down the street after dark—too many drug deals, too great a likelihood of violence.

These are uncomfortable things to write, and not just because they raise the forbidden topics of black-on-black crime and black male violence. The thing is, black men aren't *supposed* to admit to vulnerability. Hemingway's dictum about courage being grace under pressure is supposed to be the code we live by. As children we aren't just told that boys don't cry, we're encouraged to fight, and not merely to redress some childhood wrong, but

DAVID NICHOLSON

for the entertainment of older black men on street corners and sidewalks and playgrounds. We grow up learning to pretend we have no feelings. We are supposed to be cool, cooler than cool. Cold. Icemen.

I see it in the men I know who would rather watch football on television or talk about how bad Michael Jordan is than to read a book or take their children for a walk (never mind their complicity in a system that encourages black boys to gamble their lives on some precarious dream of athletic stardom). I see it in the men I know whose only contact with other black men is at work or some Thursday night basketball game where the talk is of sports, sex, cars, or stereo equipment, but not of feelings, hopes, and dreams, let alone the sharing of skills and ideas that could lead to the establishment of cooperative ventures.

And I see it in the ridiculous sight of groups of suspendered, three-piece-suited black men, all journalists, lawyers, MBAs, or government service super-grades (I live in Washington, D.C.), sitting in a downtown bar, their hard dude, side-of-the-mouth conversation liberally sprinkled with all-purpose Oedipal nouns and adjectives and references to black women as female dogs.

The thing is that times change. And if it is not yet true that we live in a colorblind society, it *is* true that we live in a world where it is worth asking whether some of the attitudes, behavior, and traits we cling to and call the core of our "culture" aren't in fact merely unproductive, self-protective ways of insisting on our difference. The issue is no longer as simple as focusing on the problems America poses for black men; we have to ask about the problems black men pose for each other and for themselves.

The questions involved here are hard but important ones, and all the more so because I want to believe that black men still have an essential role to play in the survival of blacks in America.

Our condition is desperate. Anyone who can read already knows the dismal statistics on school dropout rates, black male unemployment, the disproportionate numbers of black men in prison, and the declining numbers of black men in college. It is as if we were on a ship, some ancient vessel of dubious registry that is none too seaworthy. But there is no captain, only several who claim the right to leadership and knowledge of our course. Worse, a number of those on the ship are refusing to perform their share of the tasks that are essential if the ship is to continue to sail, hindering those who believe there might yet be a purpose, an end to this long voyage. For those black men who still believe it is worth keeping the ship afloat—even if its destination is unclear—there are some hard choices ahead.

Heretical as it may sound at a time when politically correct thinking dictates that we pretend to ignore differences, I don't think black women are going to provide the leadership black Americans need. Feminism and the new black male gay movement—both, it bears noting, indebted in tactics, strategy, and philosophy to the civil rights movement—are self-serving ideological quagmires that obscure and poison. Their theoretical tenets are based on divisive precepts all too similar to those they protest against. The popular expressions of their cause—"Abortion on Demand and Without Apology"; homosexual "art" that demands the right to celebrate in public sexual practices that ought to be private and is only a shabby excuse for pornography—leave one wondering where common sense has disappeared to. What might have been good about each movement has disappeared into some exaggerated and crippling notion of selfishness and separateness. "A woman spits," a woman I know who considers herself a feminist said once, "and we all stand around saying, 'Oh look at that. A woman spat.'"

In the same way that black women have long had their own agenda, one that thinks less of the race as a whole and more of the privilege and entitlement that can accrue to their own particular part of it, this new attention focused on black men threatens to be swept up in rhetoric and the pronouncements of charlatans.

At a 1990 conference on Afrocentric education that was

DAVID NICHOLSON

held in Atlanta, a so-called educator was challenged to explain the relevance of teaching Swahili and ancient African tribal customs to young black boys. "You are educating a man for today," he haughtily replied. "I am educating a man for eternity."

Such credulousness would be laughable if it were not so prevalent. And in the wake of this pathetic chasing after African chimeras, the hard work of devising real solutions to real problems disappears in a warm blanket of righteousness. In the end, unless black men are willing to take responsibility for their lives, this new call to examine the condition of black men in America will go wrong just as the movements that transformed American society after the civil rights movement have gone wrong—black men will insist on specialness at the expense of community, on freedom without responsibility, on privilege without duty.

The point is that black men will have to make hard choices, and precisely because we can have neither freedom without responsibility nor privilege without duty. On the communal level it seems clear that we may have to acknowledge our inability to help much of an entire generation that has grown up in a prison without walls where the strong prey on the weak and the only rule is to get over. As individuals we will have to learn how to live according to the values that have enabled us to survive and to prosper in this country—the values of discipline, hard work, sacrifice, faith both religious and secular. If this can be summed up as the notion of individual responsibility, then to it must be added the idea of imagination.

These are perhaps the quintessential American values; they are what this country has offered most of those—Native Americans are the single glaring exception—who came, willingly and unwillingly, to participate in its great experiment. At its best, America encompasses the twin notions of responsibility (the freedom to do our own thing within the context of the larger society) and imagination (the freedom not only to do and to be something different from our parents and grandparents, but to reinvent ourselves as many times as we have the energy and the

173

What It Feels Like to Be a Problem

courage to). Of course—and this is something many of us are unwilling to admit—those notions also include the possibility of failure.

For some time now, I have been thinking about what it is to be a black man and an American. Over time, I have come to believe that the roots of our present are to be found in the past.

Imagine two Africans, both men who have survived the Middle Passage and who have lived in one of the Dutch or English colonies long enough to understand that what has befallen them is not mischance or the capriciousness of fate, but a deliberate action taken by other men. The memory of their homeland remains strong, but the hope of returning to it has almost disappeared.

One man looks at his situation and thinks that he did not ask for this, does not want it, does not know how to bear it. As the months pass, he decides to endure his life, doing no more than what is demanded of him, and that only shoddily. He will rebel, malinger, cajole, dawdle.

The other considers his life and doubts that he can bear it. Yet he is responsible for others—a woman and their child. He decides to take the sliver of choice that is left him. Each time he gets a ration of corn, he saves some kernels. When his work is done, he goes to the woods. He learns how to make traps for birds and rabbits. He cuts down a small tree, makes a pole and a hook, catches fish from a stream. In the spring he plants his corn.

Though in all likelihood both men end their days as slaves, both, at the moment of their individual decisions, embark on the process of becoming Americans, transformed by their situations and the land in which they have found themselves, in much the same manner as the men who claimed the ownership of them. The difference is that one remains a victim, while the other has taken responsibility for his life.

The first slave is, of course, the "bad nigger" of fable, song, and folklore, a romantic hero for many black men, celebrated

DAVID NICHOLSON

not only in barroom and barbershop, but these days in offices and boardrooms. But it is the second man who is the *real* hero, the forebear of all the black men who plowed stony ground to harvest their crops, who drove taxis or worked in the post office so that their children could go to Morehouse or Spelman or Howard or Fisk, and so that the children of those children could go to Harvard, to Princeton, to Yale, and to the great state universities. They stayed the course. We could do worse than to emulate their courage and perseverance.

What It Feels Like to Be a Problem

Family

10. The Second Front: A Reflection on Milk Bottles, Male Elders, the Enemy Within, Bar Mitzvahs, and Martin Luther King Jr.

> Where there is no vision, the people perish.
> —Proverbs 29:18

A day does not pass when I do not brood on the negative social profile and bad PR that seem to envelop contemporary images of black males in America. As an artist and a father, I am filled with urgency and more than a little anger because I know my own son, now approaching his twenty-first birthday, and my fourteen-year-old daughter must negotiate their way through an uncivil public space soured by the steady bombardment of media images that portray black people in the worst imaginable ways—as welfare cheats, criminals, incompetent parents, ex-cons, poor students, crackheads, as an affirmative-action liability in the workplace, and, to put this bluntly, as the corrupting worm coiled inside the American apple.

I pray that my wife and I have prepared our son and daughter for the subtle and not-so-subtle shocks that will inevitably come when they are judged not, as Martin Luther King Jr. once put it, by "the content of their character" but instead by "the color of their skin." Our strategy for shoring up our kids contains no secrets—and no mythic references to the glorious triumphs of African civilizations shrouded in the dim mists of prehistory. For "civilized" models we don't need to reach back that far. From the time they were toddlers, we found as many situations as possible for putting our children in close daily contact with our predecessors (and theirs) who, despite the overly discussed victimization of black people early in this century, found ways— as Dr. Joseph Scott discusses beautifully in his memoir of a Depression-era Detroit childhood—to "make a way out of no way."

It was important to me that my son experience, firsthand and often, my own father, a man born to a large family (six boys, six girls) in South Carolina during the Great Depression because, in my opinion, he is a far better man than I'll ever be. In my early teens, he was the one black man I saw day and night, the closest example I had for measuring my own strengths and weaknesses. He became my first meditation on manhood. My challenge. My Rosetta Stone. I would sometimes study him, waiting for him to slip, which he never did, even though in the late 1950s a black criminal stole every penny he'd saved to buy our first home. (No need to elaborate on this, except to say that I watched my father lean against the doorway of the apartment where we lived, smoking his ubiquitous cigar, silent as a tree, and staring—just staring—off into space, reviewing his options after this disaster, figuring out how to make his next move.) After that loss, I watched him work three jobs in the early 1960s to support my mother and me—a day job doing construction, an evening job as a nightwatchman, and on the weekends he logged hours helping an elderly white couple fix up their house in a northshore sub-urb—a couple who remained friends of our family until their deaths. Around our house Dad was never idle, nor did he let me do much woolgathering. If he wasn't painting, he was repairing something; if he wasn't repairing something, he was planning

CHARLES JOHNSON

some improvement he intended to make (and whenever he comes to visit *my* home in Seattle, he is forever tinkering with things I've been too busy to attend to).

Not once in my life have I heard him utter an oath stronger than "Shoot!" For decades he was content to own but one carefully preserved suit, which he wore to Ebenezer A.M.E. Church, where he loved to hear the minister preach and the choir (which included a couple of my cousins) sing. Despite his workaholic habits, he told his white employers that he would do overtime and time-and-a-half on holidays, but he would never, never work on a Sunday because, as he put it, "Sunday is for church." He is always in bed by 11 P.M., up precisely at 6:30 in the morning, even nine years after retirement. A proud, quietly pious man, he paid for my college education, expecting me to acquire the professional diploma that circumstances had prevented him from getting. He'd never met any self-supporting artists of color, and so he initially opposed my desire at age fourteen to commit my life to commercial art, saying, "They don't let black people do that." He rethought his position and admitted his error when I brought him examples to the contrary, and he then paid for my lessons (via mail) with New York comic artist Lawrence Lariar, financially backing me up on something he barely understood—this, I came to see, is the very definition of love: helping others because you believe in them, regardless of whether their dreams outstrip your own understanding. When at eighteen I started saving to buy a motorcycle (I couldn't afford a car), he bought me a secondhand Corvair convertible, believing that my chances of killing myself were less likely in that than on a bike; and when I returned home from college after my first year with only the vaguest desire to get a summer job, he announced to me on my first night back that I'd better set my clock for 5 A.M., because he already had arranged three months of employment for me—as a garbage man for the city of Evanston, where he worked as a nightwatchman. He was making plans for me, I came to see, far better than I could have done myself.

And he taught me, I truly believe, *how* to work—indeed, to

179

The Second Front

see whatever I did, regardless of how humble the labor, as being a portrait of myself. And never to stop until my goal was realized. Never! To disappoint him or my mother—that I dreaded, as a boy, more than anything on earth. I cannot doubt that he learned what he knew about manhood and duty from *his* father, a farmer and blacksmith. Or that in an earlier era of black American history, his deep sense of responsibility, Protestant work ethic. and pride were widely shared by black American men. Of course, he experienced racism—my relatives in the South have ample horror stories to tell, but when I was young and eagerly probed them for every gory detail, perversely hoping to hear their personal stories about the Klan, lynchings, and the inexhaustible dirty deeds of white people, my aunts and uncles simply shook their heads and laughed, "It's better to leave that behind."

One family member who left it behind in order to keep moving forward was my father's uncle, William Johnson, whose biography I invoke often when my son and I talk late into the night or until dawn about being black men in this country. Our Uncle Will also hailed from rural South Carolina, and a life close to the land. His people farmed, spent their winters hunting, and produced nearly everything they needed. Their water came from a well. Answering nature's call in the middle of the night meant a lonely walk outside to a foul-smelling outhouse, one's feet stepping gingerly to avoid snakes. They put their children to work at age five, making them fetch things for the adults and older children as they worked. In their daily lives nothing came easily, or was taken for granted, and I am convinced that as a young man in his twenties, Uncle Will imbibed Booker T. Washington's famous program of self-reliance and his "philosophy of the toothbrush."

I remember him as a bald, dark-skinned, potbellied, suspender-wearing family patriarch (a role my father later assumed) who had a pew reserved just for him in our church (he tithed heavily), watched the evening news on his black-and-

CHARLES JOHNSON

white TV as if it were the oracle of Delphi, and loved to see his brother's kids and his great-nephews and -nieces come over for dinner in the two-story apartment building he had designed and built himself (he lived, naturally, on the top floor; he rented the first floor to a beauty parlor and barber shop, and he had his office, filled with maps, blueprints, and mysterious [to me] surveying equipment, in the basement). He told every one of us, "Get an education, that's the most important thing you can do—it's the only thing that slowed me down."

As he told the story—his own story—when Will Johnson arrived in Evanston during the Depression, he realized that white milk companies did not deliver to black people. So he started his own company in the 1930s to serve them. Under a glass globe in my living room is the last odd remnant of this commercial venture, a scarred, cloudy milk bottle that bears the inscription "One Pint. This Bottle Property of and Filled by JOHNSON DAIRY CO., Evanston, Il. Wash and Return." In a way, this innocuous, useless bottle is charged with my family's history from midcentury. It is a tissue of time and forgotten lives. On it I often perform a private hermeneutics, peeling away its layers of meaning as one would a palimpsest. I try to imagine (as archaeologists do with tools from Pompeii or shards of pottery from the Incas) how Will Johnson must have looked, early in the morning before sunrise, carrying clinking bottles like this down empty, quiet streets from one Negro family's doorstep to another, hustling to get ahead, to carve out a place for himself against the backdrop of the New Deal and a world careening toward war. I wonder how tightly the dreams of this tall, handsome, industrious black man were tied to these tiny pint containers. Did other black men tell him he was foolish to try competing with the white milk companies? Did he stay up nights wondering, like any entrepreneur, if he might fall on his face with nothing to show for his sweat and sacrifice except spilled milk? To my knowledge, no other such bottles exist. The one in my home, returned to me like a family heirloom, was

The Second Front

sealed inside the wall of a building in downtown Evanston in the thirties (whoever had it *didn't* "wash and return"). A white photographer who collected curios discovered it when the building was being remodeled in 1975; he kept it and ultimately returned it to me as a gift in 1994 in exchange for a signed copy of *Middle Passage* after I gave a commencement address at Northwestern University, one covered by the photographer, who, when I mentioned my great-uncle, thought to himself, "Say, I *have* that bottle at home."

When that milk company, those dreams, failed, Uncle Will worked on a construction crew until he learned the ropes, then, without a dime of government support, started his second business, the Johnson Construction Company, which lasted into the 1970s and is responsible for raising churches (Springfield Baptist Church), apartment buildings, and residences all over the northshore area—places where today, long after my great-uncle's death in 1989 at age ninety-seven, people still live and worship their god. In fact, once this second business took off, he was able to promise his brothers in the South jobs for their sons and daughters if they came north. My father accepted his offer, and met my mother shortly after relocating to the Chicago area, which began the chain of causation that leads forty-eight years later to this very rumination on black American men.

My son and daughter have heard me preach the preceding story often enough for it to have the effect of a sleeping pill on them. But I repeat it, mantra-like, as much for my benefit as for theirs, and primarily to remind myself that culture and civilization are but one generation deep. Yes, they can be lost in a mere twenty years. The blink of an eye. They are not givens. And if I do not tell the story of their grand- and great-grand-elders, my progeny—weaned on the less than responsible media—may forget that even in the face of staggering racial oppression (beside which today's bigotry pales), and despite the lack of opportunities in the first half of this century, our elders in the pre–civil rights era raised strong, resourceful sons and

CHARLES JOHNSON

daughters; their intention—their personal sacrifices and life-long labor—was to prepare their offspring for the chances they themselves were denied.

Black men today can do no less.

We must relearn what our elders knew regarding the primacy of the family (or extended family) as the social entity best suited for ensuring the survival of its members and providing examples of acceptable behavior for its children. We must reaffirm the need for black Americans to create their own businesses, to generate wealth and invest that wisely, as well as to instruct their children from a young age in the importance of delayed gratifi-cation, saving a portion of their earnings, and in the workings of a capitalist economy (we can carp about the evils of capital until we're blue in the face, and fantasize all day long about the Worker's Paradise, but the cold fact, to paraphrase Woodrow Wilson, is that right now and for the foreseeable future, "The business of America is business"). Lastly, we must actively work to first revitalize, then prompt the evolution of black intellec-tual, spiritual, and moral culture by challenging what the out-spoken critic Stanley Crouch has called "the enemy within."

I think you know who he means.

In fact, you may *be* who he means.

The enemy within is the black supervisor on my son's job who, after seeing that my boy doesn't do drugs or belittle women, that he is quiet and studious, a lover of chess, a martial-arts student, an aspiring writer, and the most reliable worker on his crew, derisively remarked, "I think you're a white man in a black man's body." The enemy within are the knuckle-dragging high school friends of author-journalist Nathan McCall. As he re-ports in *Makes Me Wanna Holler,* they brought their anti-intel-lectual form of peer pressure to bear upon him in exchange for his being accepted as a member of their in-crowd. "After I started hanging out," McCall writes, "the purpose of school changed completely for me. It seemed more like a social arena than someplace to learn. The academic rigors lost their luster

The Second Front

and the reward of making the honor roll just wasn't the same. Suddenly, I didn't want to be seen carrying an armload of books, and I felt too self-conscious to join in class discussions. I sat in the back of the room with the hard dudes, laughing, playing, jonin' [making fun of] the nerds."

All too often, the enemy within are the "hard dudes," the latter-day versions of Stagolee or the "bad nigger" who, once they decide to get an honest job, will in all likelihood be working for one of the driven, type-A "nerds" and wondering how in the world that happened when they, the "hard dudes," are supposed to be the ones who are too cool for the room. My father's word for them is "sorry." But the enemy within is as protean as Ralph Ellison's character Rinehart in *Invisible Man*—and just as cynical—taking numerous forms, appearing as often as a tenured professor at an Ivy League college as he does as a "hard dude." Nevertheless, the message from the enemy within is always the same: Stop trying. Don't hope. Or work for minimum wage. All you'll ever be to the rest of the world is a "savage in a suit." The system is rigged against you. Don't be so square. Why the hell you always got your nose in a book? Hey, what's with you? You don't *talk* black. What's the point of studyin' all them *white* things—you know you can't destroy the master's house with the master's tools.

Of course, the young enemy within knows nothing about Frederick Douglass's study of Roman orators to add more fire to his own speeches against slavery; he goes silent when told that Martin Luther King Jr. sat in on philosophy courses at Harvard and studied intellectual history from the pre-Socratics through Personalism at Boston University; and, despite his professed admiration for Malcolm X, he will yawn when reminded that Malcolm was fiercely moral—more so than his mentor Elijah Muhammad—and dutiful in all Muslim practices, which included meditating on his job at a furniture store after his conversion to Islam. He was overjoyed by the personal behavior he saw in others of his faith at Detroit Temple Number One: "The

CHARLES JOHNSON

men were quietly, tastefully dressed," he says in his autobiography. "The women wore ankle-length gowns, no make-up, and scarves covered their heads. The neat children were mannerly not only to adults but to other children as well." Can anyone doubt tht Malcolm X would be shocked and saddened by the sight of young black men in the nineties who adopt the trappings of prison culture—beltless trousers slung low over their behinds, their underwear showing, and the rude, harsh stares with which they meet anyone they encounter? If nothing else, Malcolm X was devoted to morally raising from the dead (as he put it) those "brainwashed black brothers and sisters, drinking, cursing, fighting, dancing, carousing, and using dope." And I believe he would be outraged by the violence of many of the "hard dudes'" rites of passage to manhood. Beatings, for example, that "jump" a young man into gang membership. On the whole, it must be said that in America we generally lack the clearly defined rites of passage that might ease young people from one stage of life to the next. Often I've wondered how different things might be if black Americans had long ago created through our churches something equivalent to the Jewish bar mitzvah, that coming-of-age ceremony in which a thirteen-year-old boy is publicly embraced as a member of the community, but only after he has spent a year in preparation, studying a lengthy section of the Torah that he will be called upon to recite before his congregation, selecting poetry or literature for this event that marks his transition from childhood—in other words, doing intellectual and cultural work to earn his respected place among others. Think about it: memorizing and reciting Psalms as a communal rite of passage has being pummeled bloody beat by a long country mile.

Down deep, the enemy within is anti-intellectual, anti-Western, anti-Christian, anti-American, and dislikes, among other things, study and the free play of the imagination and intellect. I suspect that the enemy within is also uncomfortable with Dr. King, though he (or she) may quote him to make a point about oppression, but never the King who counseled black students in Chicago in 1964 that "when you are behind in a footrace, the only way to get ahead is to run faster than the man in front of you. So when your white roommate says he's tired and goes to sleep, you stay up and burn the midnight oil."

(Put another way, we need more nerds.)

And they never quote the ethicist King who said, "We must work on two fronts. On the one hand, we must continually resist the system of segregation—the system which is the basic cause of our lagging standards; on the other hand, we must work constructively to improve the lagging standards which are the effects of segregation. There must be a rhythm of alteration between attacking the cause and healing the effects. . . . We are often too loud and boisterous, and spend too much on alcoholic beverages. These are some of the shortcomings we can improve here and now. . . . Even the most poverty stricken among us can be clean, even the most uneducated among us can have high morals. By improving these standards, we will go a long way in breaking down some of the arguments of the segregationists."

Never the King who in 1957, at the Holt Street Baptist Church, delivered a blistering speech—one he received considerable criticism for—entitled "Some Things We Must Do." On that occasion he said, "We kill each other and cut each other too much. . . . You don't need to speak good English in order to be good, but there is no excuse for our school teachers to say `you is'—they're supposed to be teaching but they're crippling our children. . . . And our doctors should not spend their time on big cars and clothes but in reading books and going to medical institutes. Too many Negro doctors have not opened a book since medical school. . . . I'm going to holler tonight because I want to get this thing over. . . . Oh, I know why Negroes like to buy Cadillacs and ride in bigger cars than whites. We've been pushed around and if we can't have a big home we can at least have a big car. But it's time to end this foolishness. There are too many Negroes with $2,000 incomes riding around in $5,000

CHARLES JOHNSON

cars." He went on to add, "The money Negroes spend on liquor in Alabama in one year is enough to endow three or four colleges. All of these things," King said, "are some things we have it in *our* power to change."

(My father, I remember, enjoyed his black, gas-guzzling, boatlike Cadillac. In fact, he had *two* of them in the late 1970s— one he later sold to our minister. But Dad also owned two homes, was financially comfortable, with his only child raised and out of the way, and after a lifetime of work his cars, of which he was very proud and which he kept spit-polish clean, were his well-earned reward to himself.)

If we had heeded King in 1958, perhaps black males might not be viewed by some today as "an endangered species." Perhaps we would, as a group, still have the reputation many of our fathers enjoyed thirty years ago—as hard-working, frugal, family-oriented Americans of faith and resilience for whom the only serious impediment to the unleashing of their genius was the despicable institution of segregation. (In other words, Colin Powell would appear as the rule, not the exception.) I am convinced as never before that after the great civil rights legislation of the 1960s, which ended legal segregation, and in today's increasingly conservative climate, whatever renewal and progress black people in America can hope for must come from *within*. This is the second "front" mentioned by King, which even he could not speak too loudly about in the sixties because he and others feared that discussing the health of our culture would only give ammunition to the enemies of integration. But we have neglected this question for too long. We need to talk about it now. Moreover, we need to *act* on it by recapturing old and developing new cultural practices worthy of the great sacrifices, intractable wills, dignity, and deep-plowing faith of our ancestors. If we do not, or for some reason cannot, we will have failed to learn the lessons so many other groups—Italians, Jews, the Chinese, West Indians, and most recently the Vietnamese boat people and Africans (who constitute 15 percent of the foreign-born black population yet have a median income $9,000 higher than that of American blacks)—have absorbed during their American odyssey, and black American males will continue to be the subject of disheartening social and economic statistics.

At this late hour in the twentieth century, 133 years after the Emancipation Proclamation, my children—and yours—deserve way better than that.

CHARLES JOHNSON

Contributors

DON BELTON, author of *Almost Midnight* and editor of *Speak My Name*, is a former reporter for *Newsweek*. He has been a fellow at MacDowell Colony, Yaddo, and the Rockefeller Center at Bellagio, Italy.

PETER J. HARRIS is editor of the Los Angeles magazine *The Drumming between Us: Love and Erotic Poetry* and has published poetry and fiction since the 1970s.

CHARLES JOHNSON won the National Book Award for Fiction in 1990 for *Middle Passage*. He is the author of several novels, including *Oxherding Tale* and *Faith and the Good Thing;* a collection of stories, *The Sorcerer's Apprentice;* and *Being and Race: Black Writing since 1970*.

DR. WILBERT JORDAN is a specialist in infectious diseases and directs the AIDS program at the King-Drew Medical Clinic in Los Angeles.

YUSEF KOMUNYAKAA was the recipient of the 1994 Pulitzer Prize in poetry. He is currently on leave from Indiana University in Bloomington.

JACOB LAWRENCE was born in 1917 and began his career in New York City in the late 1930s. Within a decade his contribution to modern American and African American art began to be recognized. His work has been featured in three major retrospective exhibitions since 1960. He is a member of the American Academy of Arts and Letters and a recipient of the National Medal of Arts. Lawrence currently lives and works in Seattle, Washington.

ELLIS MARSALIS is a jazz pianist/composer and Director of the Jazz Studies Division at the University of New Orleans.

JOHN McCLUSKEY, JR., teaches Afro-American literature and fiction writing at Indiana University–Bloomington. He is the author of two novels, *Look What They Done to My Song* and *Mr. America's Last Season Blues,* and the editor of *The City of Refuge: Collected Stories of Rudolph Fisher.* His short fiction has appeared in a number of journals and anthologies. *The River People* is the title of his novel in progress.

DAVID NICHOLSON is an assistant editor of the *Washington Post Book World* and the founding editor of the magazine *Black Film Review.* His short stories have been published in literary magazines, and he is the author of a novel, *Seasons,* about Negro League baseball players.

MICHAEL O'NEAL is the founder and president of Fathers, Inc., and a community activist in Boston.

JOSEPH W. SCOTT is Professor of Sociology and Professor of American Ethnic Studies at the University of Washington at Seattle. He is the author of *The Black Revolts: Racial Stratification in the United States* and has published more than thirty-five articles on American race and ethnic relations, the African American family, and criminal justice. He is the father of two daughters and a son.

Contributors